To: Mexxa
 I hope that th
you a greater revelat
In love God so much.
me.

Althea Dixon

When Night Turns Into Morning

When Night Turns Into Morning

Althea Lee Dixon

Copyright © 2011 by Althea Lee Dixon.

Library of Congress Control Number: 2011903737
ISBN: Hardcover   978-1-4568-8430-7
                Softcover   978-1-4568-8429-1
                Ebook   978-1-4568-8431-4

All rights reserved. No part of this book may be reproduced or transmitted in any form or by any means, electronic or mechanical, including photocopying, recording, or by any information storage and retrieval system, without permission in writing from the copyright owner.

This book was printed in the United States of America.

To order additional copies of this book, contact:
Xlibris Corporation
1-888-795-4274
www.Xlibris.com
Orders@Xlibris.com
94140

CONTENTS

Foreword 9
Acknowledgments 11
Introduction 13

Chapter 1 Look Outside the Box...15
Chapter 2 Don't Get Bitter Because of the Process 38
Chapter 3 Say Goodbye to the Past 57
Chapter 4 Dreams and Visions..76
Chapter 5 Disappointments 102
Chapter 6 Does God Always Meet Our Needs? 126
Chapter 7 How To Forgive The Unthinkable! 142
Chapter 8 Beauty For Ashes 167

End Notes 191
About the Author 195
Index 197

Dedication

To my Lord and Savior Jesus Christ, for without him, I am nothing. And to my husband and best friend, Raffleton, of twenty-seven years, who is always in my corner, loving and supporting me unconditionally. To my three children and personal fan club, Shea-Marie, Jordan, and Philip, who cheered me on every time I felt like giving up on the writing of this book. Also to my mother, Cyriline Lee, who has always encouraged me to dream big and trust God with everything! Last, but not least, to the stranger from Texas named Tim. Tim, you gave me the title to my book during an early morning conversation on a cruise ship in 2007. Tim, you told me how you loved to wake up early each morning just to see when night turns into morning.

FOREWORD

The very last day before my mom was to submit this manuscript for publication, she burst into my bedroom like a tornado and woke me up. At first, I immediately jumped to the conclusion that something was terribly wrong! But when she asked if I could do her a favor, I realized that there weren't any immediate threats—like the house was on fire or she needed to go to the hospital. I foolishly said, "Yes"—not knowing what she wanted. I thought she wanted me to wash the dishes or clean the bathroom or make her a cup of her favorite lemon and honey tea—that she religiously drank every day. Actually, I wish that it was one of those chores she wanted me to do because when she finally told me what she wanted, I almost fell out of bed. She asked me if I would write the foreword for her book. I didn't even know what a "foreword" was. I had to look it up. Then, when I kind of got the general idea what it meant, I didn't have the slightest clue where to begin. But I must confess that I felt honored that my mother would trust me enough to ask. I know how much this book means to her—it was a huge undertaking for her.

Over the past three years since she's been writing this book, my mom has gone through a lot more heartaches and pain. No wonder why she decided to write a book. She's an expert on pain. If you look up the word, "pain" in the dictionary, you would see a picture of my mother. It's unbelievable how much one person can endure so much hardship and still have a positive outlook on life. Over the past four years, my relationship with my mother has changed. We went from being mother and daughter to being best friends. It's funny how pain can sometimes draw people closer. In 2007, during a trip to Jamaica, a dear friend of hers did something to hurt her. It broke her heart. She came back that year changed! Unfortunately, that same year, I had to go away to college, so I wasn't home as often as I would have liked. We talked almost every day on the telephone. It was my way of keeping an eye on her because I knew that she needed a friend.

Then one day, the unthinkable happened. In the midst of my mother's suffering, she suffered a ruptured brain aneurysm and became very ill. Just when I thought that things couldn't get any worse, it did! By this time, I had just finished college and had just started a new job. When the time came for my mom to be discharged from the hospital, she needed someone to take care of her and I was the most likely candidate. I had to quit my new job, pack up my belongings, and move back home, leaving my boyfriend and my younger brother, Jordan, behind. My mom needed me, and I needed to be there for her. She had been there for me my entire life and now; it was my turn to give back.

The recuperation period was a nightmare! She was in so much pain that it pained me to watch her suffer. I felt helpless! She cried herself to sleep every night for months. One night, while we were up waiting for her pain medication to kick in, she asked me if I thought that she would ever get better and if she would ever be herself again. I told her that this would only be for a season and that this too shall pass. I cannot count all the times my mom used those very words to encourage me during the most difficult times in my life. I considered it a privilege that God would use me to use those same words to pour back into her. Now—it has been more than a year since her surgery, and my mom is stronger than she's ever been—spiritually. Her passion and thirst for God and life has truly been inspiring. The world can take a page out of her book and I mean that literally! It is my prayer that this book which was birthed out of pain and suffering would encourage the hearts of the readers just as much as my mother and best friend has encouraged me my entire life.

Shea-Marie Dixon

ACKNOWLEDGMENTS

Most credited authors have a long list of people whom they give acknowledgments to in the writing of their book. In my case, I only have three.

To my niece, Tiffany who has been my invaluable writing mentor and sounding board during the entire process of this manuscript. She was extremely instrumental in transferring the contents of my journal unto the computer. Being a computer technology illiterate and a two-finger typist, I didn't even know how to turn on the computer when I first started. Tiffany was my English teacher, research specialist, and late-night companion when I was up writing into the wee hours of the morning. Her constant encouragement and faith-filled words helped me to envision the completion of this book.

And to my husband who went to bed alone many nights for three years while I sat at the computer until my neck, back, and head hurt. Who did a lot of the cooking when we wanted a home-cooked meal instead of fast foods and microwave dinners, and he never complained not even once when I didn't have the time to cuddle up with him on the sofa, like we always did, and watch a movie.

And to my family who filled in the blanks in my memory after I suffered a brain aneurysm and couldn't remember a lot of my past.

INTRODUCTION

The writing of this book was inspired by a dream that I had in 2007 that ignited a fire in my belly to share with you how God healed me repeatedly of heart wounds—wounds that went way beyond my shattered heart and into my soul. Ever since I was a child, I would dream often. In the beginning, I thought nothing of it until my dreams started to come to pass. Soon, I came to realize that it was definitely a gift from God and not the colorful imagination of a child.

In my dreams, I would see graphic events of my life and the lives of others. The dream that actually inspired the writing of this book was more like a nightmare. But upon awakening, I knew that it was more than just an ordinary dream. I knew that it had a valuable message. At first, I didn't have a clue what the interpretation was until about a week later when I was visiting with my mother. I was confiding in her about a very painful situation that I was going through and had been for several years. I found myself weeping frenziedly as I was desperately trying to explain to her the deep emotional anguish that was raging in my soul.

It was then my mother told me to get a journal and start writing down all my thoughts. Since writing was already one of my many passions, I immediately felt encouraged to start journalizing my pain. I was quickly amazed as to how therapeutic writing had become for me, and soon, my journal was turning into a book. The more I poured myself out on paper, the more I felt Jesus guiding and comforting me through the pain. In writing this book, I wrote myself out of the belly of depression, and as I penned each word, phrase, sentence and paragraph, I saw the shackles on my wrists, just like I had seen them in my dream, turn into plastic and burst asunder.

I still consider my life a work in progress, and maybe always will, but my sole intention in writing this book is to show you how God can carry you through unthinkable circumstances—through the death of a loved one, sickness, rejection, betrayal, depression, shame, disappointments . . . or whatever circumstances you might be facing in your life. My prayer is that God would use this book and the stories in it to develop your faith to trust Him to do the impossible.

If you're in the furnace of affliction and you don't see a way out, I want to introduce you to the greatest navigator of all. His name is Jesus Christ. Eric Liddell (an Olympian) said, "Circumstances may appear to wreck our lives and God's plans, but God is not helpless among the ruins." Disappointments and failures are a part of life; it's inevitable, but to lose hope and give up in despair is not. That's a choice! You have the right to lie down and die if that is what you choose or to get up and shake your fist in the devil's face and live. It's solely up to you.

There were so many times in my life when I didn't want to get up and live. I wanted to curl up into a little ball somewhere and die. I felt helpless among the ruins, but God wasn't! God showed me that He wasn't impotent in my sufferings, just silent. Sometimes we mistake God's silence in our circumstances as a lack of love on His part. But that's not the case at all. God is always at work behind the scenes in our lives whether we recognize it or not.

As I learned to let go of the ashes by relinquishing my pain into God's hands, God took the ashes and gave me beauty instead. As I take you step-by-step into the most intimate, secret places of my life, I will show you how God used my shame and disappointments as learning tools to mold and shape me into the kind of vessel that He could use to further his kingdom. In the end, I finally realized that obedience is truly better than sacrifice.

CHAPTER 1

Look Outside the Box

For His anger is but for a moment, His favor is for life; Weeping may endure for a night, but joy comes in the morning.
—Psalms 30:4 (New King James)

Ever since I was a little girl, I have always believed in fairy tales and puppy dog tales. I was a dreamer. Always dreaming of love and totally in love with the idea of love. Always looking for that silver lining and the "happily ever after" ending to every love story. I had my ideal husband picked out when I was only five, and I wasn't picky either. As long as he was the male version of me—romantic, funny, and of course, a dreamer—I was satisfied. So when I met my husband at a Kitchener house party on June 22, 1980, I was absolutely certain that it wasn't him. It wasn't love at first sight at all. Not even like. My husband accompanied one of his friends from another city, Hamilton, where he lived, seventy kilometers west to Kitchener, where I lived, to attend a house party.

I went with one of my friends to the party that night not knowing I was going to meet the man that I would eventually marry. Do you believe that everything happens for a reason? Do you believe in destiny? I do! What would have happened if my husband hadn't accompanied his friend to Kitchener that night? Come to find out later that my husband was invited to come to Kitchener many times in the past but declined. He told me that he didn't think that a small, provincial city had any good-looking girls—only a bunch of country bumpkins. But the first time he agreed to go was the night he met his wife. I, on the other hand, wasn't even planning on going out that night. If my friend hadn't called and convinced me to go . . . well, you know what happened.

My husband, Raffleton, a.k.a. Black Terror, was a high-energy DJ and rapper. He was rapping that night and I hated his lyrics. It was negative and disrespectful to women—just inappropriate! I even sent a message to him, through one of my friends, to tell him to stop talking trash about women. We didn't talk at all that night until about a month later when I ran into him, again, at another house party and he asked me to dance. That was over thirty years ago. In the beginning, it was a hit-and-miss kind of relationship. On our first date after I introduced him to my mother, she told me to get rid of him. Actually, that night, I took my pregnant sister with me on our first date. That's how much I trusted this guy. Nobody in my family approved of him for me. They all thought that he wasn't tall, handsome, and good enough for me. In the beginning, I took a lot of flak for being with him. Although my family didn't tell him to his face what they thought about him, he knew. On the other hand, his family didn't have a problem with me. They thought that I was beautiful. On our first date when I was about to tell him that I didn't want to go out with him again, Dixon, that's what he told me to call him, said the strangest thing. He said, "I know I'm not good looking, but I have a good heart." I think that was when I took a second look, and thank God I did!

We dated for three years before we got married, and during those years, we struggled. My husband was a mama's boy! No matter what his mother told him to do, he would do it. I remember a quarrel that we had once, and he told me off good and proper. He said, "I can always find another girlfriend if I want, but I have only one mother." I replied, "That's fine, then you shouldn't have a problem dating your mother." I was ready to dump his little five feet four inches—OK, maybe five feet five inches—mama's boy(you know what) when he apologized. If anyone had told me that we would have lasted over thirty years and become the best of friends, like we are today, I would have laughed in their face. We both came from the same country—Jamaica—but we were as different as night and day.

I was a city girl from a middle class family, and he was a country bumpkin from a poor family. I was romantic, and he wasn't. I was a dreamer, and he was a realist. I loved going to the movies. He loved going to parties. I loved the theater. He loved going to parties. I loved romantic weekends in Niagara Falls. He loved going to parties. Need I say more—after all, he was a DJ. We were the two people who most likely wouldn't have ended up together. We literally had to bend, almost break, during the courtship, but the one thing that kept us together was love. In our case, I guess, it's true what they say, love really does conquer all. We loved each other, and over time, our love blossomed. When we decided to marry, we had very little money, but we didn't want to wait until we had enough money for a big splashy wedding. We knew what we had was the real thing, and that was more than enough to build a lifetime on. My engagement ring cost $50, but to me, it was priceless! I couldn't afford a proper wedding dress, much more to take a honeymoon, but we also knew that things weren't always going to be that way forever. We knew that it was going to be hard, at first, but if we worked hard and watch each other's backs, we would be all right.

We lived with my mother, after my father left her for another woman, until my father came back three years later and threw all of us out of the house. My father demanded his share of the house, forcing my mother to either buy him out or put up the house for sale. We couldn't afford to buy him out, so we had to put up the house for sale. After the house was sold, we all split up and moved into separate apartments. Our first home as a married couple was a small apartment, but it was ours, and it was home. It was the first time we had ever been alone in three years of marriage. But that would soon change again, this time for the better.

Only a couple of months later, I found out that I was pregnant with our first child. It was one of the most incredible feelings I had ever experienced. I had been trying to conceive for three years, but I couldn't! Since I had only one ovary and one fallopian tube as a result of a miscarriage I had when I was seventeen years old; my chances of becoming pregnant were slim to nothing. Suddenly, one night, I was rushed to the hospital emergency room, with stomach pains. It was there, upon examination, the doctor told me that I was pregnant. Not exactly the way I had envisioned telling my husband that he was going to become a father for the first time, but nevertheless, it was implausible!

The pregnancy was tremendously difficult, to say the least. Because this was my first, I didn't know what was normal and what wasn't. I soon realized it was normal to have morning sickness when you are pregnant, but mine was severe. Bleeding was not considered normal during pregnancy, so when I started bleeding, I was immediately hospitalized. The entire nine months was hell! I didn't have one normal day throughout the entire pregnancy. But after nine dreadful months and twenty-three hours of unbearable labor pains, I gave birth to the most beautiful, perfect baby girl in the world, and she was worth it. Seven pounds, four ounces of pure joy was placed in my arms by my husband. He was right there in the delivery room with me when I gave birth to all five of our children, including a set of twins.

He never left my side, not even for a second. Not even when my daughter was diagnosed at three months with a heart defect. He was there for every doctor's appointment, every sleepless night—even though he had to get up early for work the next day. He was there when the doctors were talking about performing heart surgery on a three-month-old baby. My husband, and now, my best friend, was there for me during every storm in our marriage; for better or worse, in sickness and health, he was there. Dixon embodies the very heart of Christ. He's Christlike in so many ways. This man whom everyone swore wasn't good enough for me because he wasn't tall enough or handsome enough, and his skin color wasn't light enough—yeah, you heard right. Everyone said he was too dark for me. Never judge a book by its cover. This little man turned out to be a giant among men and the best thing that had ever happened to me.

How is it possible for two people from two different worlds to become one flesh? Bruce Lee said, "Love is like a friendship caught on fire: In the beginning a flame, very pretty, often hot and fierce, but still only light and flickering. As love grows older, our hearts mature and our love become as coals, deep-burning and unquenchable." Indeed, there's nothing more beautiful than two friends in love with one another. That's what Dixon and I have—a friendship caught on fire! But it wasn't always that way. In the beginning, it wasn't very pretty. Neither was it hot and fierce. It took a while before I understood the words of author Janette Oke, who wrote in one of her novels, "Love isn't always fireworks. Sometimes love just comes softly."

Sometimes love takes time. And in our case, it took a long time. Let's face it, every relationship goes through the fire—the refiner's fire! But not all comes forth like gold—ours did! Every person on this planet is going to go through hard times. It's inevitable! And every relationship is going to be tested. Whether the relationship is platonic or sexual, it's going to be tested. The refiner's fire is the difficulties that we go through. It's symbolic for the hurts, disappointments, rejections, betrayals, death, divorce, etc., that we must face. One of the most painful refiner's fire experiences of my entire life happened on August 4, 1988.

Refiner's Fire

"Weeping may endure for a night, but joy comes in the morning." One afternoon in July 1988, Jesus appeared to me in a dream and spoke those exact words. At that time, I was five months pregnant with twins. After four months of severe nausea, vomiting, and bleeding, I thought, for sure, that the worst was over. I thought that the storm clouds were finally disappearing, and for the first time since I heard my doctor say, "Congratulations! Althea, you're pregnant," I could actually see the sun peeking through the clouds again.

I was already a young mother to a beautiful seventeen-month-old baby girl named, Shea-Marie, and now, I was expecting twins, two boys. Everything was perfect! Everything was right in the universe—so I thought! But in the real world, there is no such thing. I was extremely sick with the pregnancy, far more than I had been with my first. I was hospitalized so many times that I was certain that God was upset with me about something. Actually, that's how I found out I was expecting twins. It was during one of my many hospitalizations that I first learned of it.

For as long as I can remember, I had always wanted to have twins, not just twins, but twin boys. So you can just imagine how thrilled I was when my doctor walked into my hospital room and told me that I was pregnant with twins. I thought for sure that I was delusional from all the medications that I was taking. But after a while, she convinced me that I wasn't. At that moment, I thought that I had died and gone to heaven. The news took my breath away. It was truly awesome! My mother was the first person I called after the doctor left the room. I had to tell her first because she knew more than anyone else how badly I wanted twins. It was my mother who inadvertently started me on the quest to have twins.

As I recall, I must have been about five years old when I said to God, "God, when I grow up, I want to be the mommy of twins." I was playing with two little black dolls on the veranda of our small two-bedroom, one-outhouse, and no-indoor-plumbing house that my father built. One of the dolls belonged to my sister, Rose, and the other was mine. It was then that I said something that would change my life forever; whether it was the sincere prayer of a child or the foolish ramblings of a dreamer, only time would tell. I first conceived the idea of twins from my mother, Cyriline, and her twin sister, Gladys, who everyone calls, Tiny. She was called Tiny because she was so tiny at birth compared to my mother.

My mother and Auntie Tiny are fraternal twins, but they look so much alike that the moment you see them together, you know that they have to be twins. I remember how curious I was when my mother sat me down and tried to explain what twins are. It was hilarious! But in everything that she said, the one thing that stood out the most was how her mother, Grandma

Sarah, carried her and Auntie Tiny in her tummy at the same time. I just couldn't fathom someone walking around with two tiny human beings inside of them for nine months. It was unbelievable! That was the day a tiny seed was sown into the heart of a child that germinated over time and blossomed into a dream, a dream that I carried in my heart and soul for over twenty years.

Now, I was twenty-eight years old, and I was carrying two tiny human beings inside my tummy, just like Grandma Sarah. God had finally answered my prayers. Imagine, twenty-three years later, and I was living my dream. My dream was not just a dream anymore; it had come true. The pregnancy was progressing quite nicely, and all I could think about was the day when I would hold my babies in my arms for the first time. I was consumed with thoughts of what it would feel like to hug them and kiss them and look into their tiny faces to see if I could catch a glimpse of myself in their eyes. I must have thanked God a thousand times for answering my prayers. I had so many plans for my children, like all parents do, but tragedy was lurking in the shadows like a predator waiting to pounce on its prey.

A Midsummer Day's Dream

Then suddenly, one afternoon, Jesus appeared to me in a dream and told me something that would change my life forever. It wasn't until the day of the twin's funeral when I heard the pastor say, "Weeping may endure for a night, but joy comes in the morning," that I finally understood what God was trying to tell me. He had already walked into my tomorrow and saw the premature deaths of my children. The dream was a warning. I believe that sometimes God will warn us of impending danger, but quite often, we miss the warning signs out of ignorance.

Look at the story in Genesis 19 about the destruction of Sodom and Gomorrah. God sent two angels into Sodom and Gomorrah to warn a man named Lot. The people were so vile and their hearts deceitfully wicked that God wanted to wipe them off the face of the earth. But because of one man, Lot, whom God loved, He didn't think that it would be fair for him and his family to get caught in the cross fire. So God made arrangements to get Lot and his family out of the city before He pronounced judgment upon the inhabitants. When Jesus appeared to me in my dream that afternoon, it was to warn me, but I didn't heed the warning. I didn't understand, and as a result, I lost something really precious to me. I had never felt so much pain in my entire life like I did on August 4, 1988. That was the day when my twins were born, and that was the day when they died.

In twelve hours, it felt like my entire world had evaporated right before my eyes. I went from being one of the happiest women in the world to being the saddest. My beautiful baby boys were dead. They lived only twelve hours. For twelve hours, my lifelong dream became tangible. I saw it. I handled it. It was real! Was it a part of God's will? Were they predestined to just make a brief appearance into this world, say hello, and then goodbye? Those twelve hours changed my life forever. Their brief manifestation made a huge difference in all of our lives. Two tiny people, so tiny, that they shared the same tomb—like they shared the same womb. I remember when my husband and I were making the funeral arrangements and the funeral director suggested that we purchase only one casket for both of them. I must confess that I was deeply offended by his suggestion until he explained to us that the babies were so tiny that they could easily fit into one casket. He also said that if we were to bury them together, they would always be together. Although it was a poor attempt to comfort us in our time of grief, we knew that his heart was in the right place. To be perfectly honest, I would have believed anything he told me just as long as it gave me the strength that I needed to get through the funeral.

But on the day of the funeral, standing over this little gold-and-white shoe-box-size casket that housed the bodies of my precious babies, I wasn't feeling very nostalgic at all. All I kept saying to myself was, "Why, Lord, why?" I went into the hospital full, full of hopes, full of dreams, full of joy, but I came out empty. It was then I knew what Naomi must have felt like in Ruth 1:20-21 when she said, "Do not call me Naomi; call me Mara (Mara means bitterness): for the Almighty has dealt very bitterly with me. I went out full, and the Lord has brought me home again empty. Why do you call me Naomi, since the Lord has testified against me, and the Almighty has afflicted me?" I too felt like God had afflicted me and that He had testified against me. I was angry! And I stayed angry for a very long time.

I want you to stop for a moment and think of a time in your life when you prayed desperately for something, something that you wanted so badly that you could actually taste it. Like that promotion at work that you've been working yourself to death for. Or maybe that business you've always wanted to own so that you wouldn't have to put up with people bossing you around all the time. Or maybe you are single and you've been praying for what seems like forever for that ideal spouse only to watch others get married for the second or even the third time while you're still waiting on

God. Then one day you finally get it. God came through for you in such a big way, and you are ecstatic. You feel like you're on top of the world, and it feels marvelous! Then all of a sudden, you lose it—ripped right out of your hands, sifted through your fingers like sand. That's exactly how I felt the day my babies died.

The morning I was discharged from the hospital, I remember the nurse pushing my wheelchair down the hallway to the elevators and out the emergency entrance. Apparently it was the hospital's policy for patients leaving the hospital to be transported by wheelchair to their cars. My husband was carrying my suitcase, and I was supposed to be carrying my babies. That's how I had envisioned it. That day was supposed to be one of the happiest days of my life, but it wasn't. Instead, it turned out to be one of the darkest days of my entire life. My arms were supposed to be full, holding my two little bundles of joy, but they weren't. My arms were empty! The wheelchair ride to my car felt like I was going to the gas chamber rather than going home. It wasn't supposed to turn out like this; it was supposed to have a happy ending. My babies were dead, and all my hopes and dreams died along with them. My dream was covered up underneath a blanket in the hospital's morgue. I remembered saying to myself on the ride home, "God, I can't do this. This is more than I can bear."

For months, I cried myself to sleep every night. My arms ached to hold my babies. I felt empty and dead inside. I kept replaying the events of their death over and over again in my mind, wondering what I could have done differently. It felt like a nightmare, except that I wasn't asleep. It felt like a sick, cruel joke, and the joke was on me—for believing that something good could ever happen to someone like me. The grief was like a consuming fire shot up in my bones. It was unlike anything I had ever experienced before. I thought the pain would never end. I felt swallowed up in this darkness. It was insufferable!

It reminded me of another story in the Bible about a man name Jonah. In the book of Jonah, Jonah was swallowed alive by a whale, and he spent three days in the belly of the whale. I must have heard that story a million times while I was growing up, but I never believed it. Nobody can survive being swallowed alive for three days. *That's impossible!* I thought. But you can't believe some parts of the Bible while rejecting others. It's impractical. You must embrace or reject the whole book. Jonah must have thought that it was all over for him—lights out. He must have thought that he was fish food and he would never see the light of day again. That's how I felt (not the fish food part), but I thought that I would never feel whole again.

I had all these questions racing through my mind but never knowing what the answers were. I would lie awake at night for hours questioning God and demanding answers from Him. And when I didn't get any, I would throw these temper tantrums like a two-year-old until I became exhausted and fall asleep. I wondered, "Oh God, what did I do that was so terrible that you would punish me this way?" Then, I started thinking about all the terrible things that I had done from the day I was born up to that moment. It was like someone had pressed the rewind button in my mind, and I was reliving the past all over again, but in slow motion. I thought about the time when I got pregnant at seventeen years old and almost died. Now, that was a mistake that could have been fatal if God hadn't intervened.

It was the summer of 1976, and I had just miraculously completed grade 11. I said miraculously because, in those days, high school graduates were as rare as winning the lottery. I was only seventeen years old and already involved with a man ten years my senior. He was the cousin of my best friend, and I was in love—so I thought! Looking back now through a more mature pair of eyes, I just cannot comprehend what I saw in that man. Not only was he way too old for me, it was unlawful for a twenty-seven-year-old man to be sexually involved with a seventeen-year-old girl. I should have told my parents about the relationship so that they could have protected me against this predator. Or better yet, I shouldn't have gotten involved with him at all.

Being a teenager was a very confusing period in my life. Legally, I was still a minor. I was only seventeen. But on the other hand, I was only one year away from what the law stipulates as being an "adult." I didn't want to wait until I turned eighteen. I thought that eighteen was just a number. You know what, it is just a number! Not because you're eighteen years old means that you're mature enough to make adult decisions. Maturity comes over time; it's a process. Not a number! Author Marie Ebner von Eschenbach said, "In youth we learn; in age we understand." I wish that I would have given myself time to grow up slowly and normally, the way children ought to and definitely the way God had intended. Children should be children for as long as they can. It's hard enough being an adult as it is.

Some days, most adults don't even know which way is up. And if the truth be told, some of us adults would give an arm and a leg to be a child again. It's not all fun and games like we see in magazines and on television. Children seem to be in a hurry to grow up so that they can drink alcohol, smoke cigarettes, and have sex. They think it's "sick" like my children call it nowadays. Back when I was a teenager, it was "cool." But whether it's "sick" or "cool," it was certainly not responsible behavior for a seventeen-year-old to be having sex with a twenty-seven-year-old man. No wonder why the world is in such a crisis, spinning out of control and heading for destruction. There is nothing purer and more precious than the innocence of a child, and that innocence should be protected at any cost. But unfortunately, mine wasn't! I lost my innocence a long time ago, long before I had allowed a twenty-seven-year-old man to violate me and steal my virginity.

Suffer the Little Children

I lost my innocence when I was seven years old. I never thought that I would ever be free to talk about what I'm about to. But thanks be to God who makes it possible for us to triumph in the face of adversities. My parents had tenants living next door to us when I was growing up. It was a couple that had rented a house that my family owned. They had to be in their early to midtwenties at the time, and they had no children. As I recall, they weren't married either. They were living together in a common-law relationship like most of the couples in the community. I liked them. They seemed like nice people, and I trusted them. Then again, I was nine years old. I was a child, and like all children, I trusted everyone. This couple was friends of my parents, so whenever they invited me to come over to their house, my parents didn't have a problem with it. But what my parents didn't know was that this man wasn't such a good friend after all. Actually, he was a very bad man. I migrated to Canada when I was thirteen years old, and it was shortly after that, during adolescence, I started having flashbacks of things that he had done to me as a child. Awful things!

In the beginning, I didn't have a clue what the flashbacks were all about. I thought that they were figments of my imagination. It wasn't until after I started having sex at seventeen years old, I realized that something terrible had happened to me. The images of these bad sexual acts that were perpetrated on me were like bits and pieces of a jigsaw puzzle in my mind, but I wasn't able to put them together. I had always had a vague recollection of the abuse when I was growing up, but a lot of the details were foggy and almost didn't seem real. They were like nightmares. For a long time, even to this day, I wouldn't let anyone touch my genitals, not even my husband. I would become very uncomfortable and easily agitated whenever anyone attempted to. Because of that, my first sexual experience was very awkward.

I wouldn't allow penetration at all. I wasn't uncomfortable because of the normal discomfort that is associated with losing your virginity. I knew enough about sex to know that having sex for the first time is painful. That wasn't what I was experiencing. What I was experiencing was more like repulsion and shame. I hated being touched in certain places and in certain ways, but I didn't know why. After I realized that the flashbacks were authentic, and I was sexually abused as a child, I knew that I had to tell someone in order to make it real. Although I knew that I should have told someone in the beginning, I didn't! I was afraid that no one would believe me. This man was a close friend of the family. I thought that if I were to tell my parents what their friend was doing to me, they wouldn't believe me and I would probably get into trouble and be disciplined for it. So I kept my mouth shut. And as a result, the abuse continued a lot longer than it should have.

For those of you who are going through or went through something similar to what I went through and you haven't told anyone, I would encourage you to seek out someone whom you can trust and break the silence. Whether you talk to a professional or a friend, it doesn't matter—just talk to someone! I found that by keeping the abuse a secret, I kept giving my abuser power over me, thus enabling him to continue the abuse for as long as he wanted. I was protecting him from being held accountable for his actions. My silence kept him from being prosecuted to the fullest extent of the law. In other words, he got away with it! It took a long time to break the silence. I was twenty-four years old when I broke the silence and told someone. My husband was the first person I trusted enough to tell, and when I finally told him, he wasn't surprise at all. He told me that he had always known that something was wrong, but he was waiting on me to come to him whenever I was ready. If it hadn't been for my husband who lovingly and patiently helped me to overcome the guilt and shame that destroyed all of my relationships up to that point and almost destroyed my marriage, I would still be that frightened little girl that couldn't speak up for herself.

Shortly after I told my husband, he encouraged me to tell my parents. So after a lifetime had gone by, I finally told my mother. She wept bitterly! Of all the thoughts and questions that must have been racing through her mind at that moment, she only asked me one question. She wanted to know why I didn't tell her about the abuse while it was happening to me. I didn't have the heart to tell her that I was afraid that she wouldn't believe me. Unfortunately, I know women who came forward and spoke up about being sexually abused by a friend of the family or even by another family member only to have their own family accused them of lying or worse—of doing something wrong. What could a child possibly do wrong to encourage an adult to molest him or her? Absolutely nothing! It took me a lot longer to finally open up to my father. That was extremely painful. By the time I told him, I was forty-four years old, and my parents had been divorced for many years. No wonder why I was so messed up as a teenager.

Pregnant at Seventeen

I was only seventeen years old when I found out that I was pregnant with my first child. Instead of dreaming about who was going to take me to my high school prom or which college I wanted to attend, there I was trying to figure out how to tell my parents that I was pregnant and pregnant for a twenty-seven-year-old man who had already fathered three children by two different women. What does that say about the path that I was on? And if that wasn't bad enough, this man was a fugitive hiding from the immigration department. He was eventually arrested and deported back to Jamaica within weeks after I found out that I was pregnant. Ironically, I found out that I was pregnant the same day that he was arrested. Actually, I was sitting in the police station waiting for information about his arrest when I called home and my mother told me that the doctor had called and informed her that I was pregnant. My mother didn't even know that I had gone to see my doctor. She was distraught! I still remember the look of pain and disappointment I saw in her eyes when I got home and told her everything. I thought that she was going to have a nervous breakdown. On the other hand, my father wanted to put a beating on this man real badly. But since he was already incarcerated, I begged my dad to let it go.

The next several weeks following the news of my pregnancy were difficult, to say the least. By then the father of my baby was gone, and I didn't know what I was going to do. Although this loser knew that I was pregnant before he was deported, I never heard a word from him for many years. He left a seventeen-year-old pregnant girl to fend for herself! It would be six years before I ever saw his worthless, pathetic face again. I can't describe the fear that gripped my heart when I realized that I was a child having a child. I thought to myself, "How in the world am I going to take care of a baby?" I didn't even know how to care for myself or else I wouldn't be in such a predicament. Then suddenly, late one night, I became very ill and was rushed to the hospital by my older brother, Anthony. After I was examined in the emergency room, the doctor told me that I had suffered a miscarriage and had to be hospitalized overnight for a simple dilation and curettage (D&C) procedure. But what was about to happen would change my life forever! After the procedure, I was on my way back to my room when I started hemorrhaging. Unbeknown to the doctor, the pregnancy was ectopic. My left fallopian tube had ruptured spewing amount of blood into my stomach. What was supposed to be a simple procedure turned into an emergency surgery to save my life!

There were extensive damages to both the fallopian tubes and left ovary. In order to save my life, the surgeon had to remove my left ovary and tube, but my right ovary was still intact. On the contrary, my right fallopian tube was severely damaged—but salvageable. After the surgery, I woke up to my family keeping vigil at my bedside. Their faces painted a grim picture of my true condition and why I was in so much pain when I tried sitting up in the bed. As soon as I lifted up my hospital gown and saw a huge bandage across my abdomen, I knew that something terrible had happened to me. My family was about to explain what had happened when the surgeon walked in and asked everyone to leave so that he could examine me. He explained how he almost had to remove both ovaries and both tubes in order to save my life, but when he took into consideration that I was only seventeen years old, with my entire life still in front of me, he felt obligated to do whatever he could to give me a chance to have children one day. He repaired the right fallopian tube, gave me a blood transfusion, and told me that I had a slim chance of ever becoming pregnant.

Although I was grief stricken, I knew in my heart that losing the pregnancy was for the best. Right now, you must be thinking, "How in the world could anyone in their right mind think that losing a child is for the best? I said that because, in my case, it was for the best. Clearly, I wasn't mature enough to raise a child all by myself. Please don't misunderstand what I am saying. I don't support abortion and never will. But at seventeen years old, I was a child, and I was nowhere close to becoming a parent, especially a single parent. Children need to have two parents that will love and provide a stable environment for them. I wouldn't have been able to give that to my baby, and eventually, my parents would have had that unexpected burden placed upon them. Sometimes, when bad things happen, they happen for the right reasons; just because we don't understand why doesn't mean that God is not in control. Life has an amazing way of unraveling its mysteries, and before we know it, we finally come face-to-face with the truth. I still don't know why I had to go through all that, and maybe I never will, but the painful lessons that I have learned from the mistakes of my past, I wouldn't trade that knowledge for anything.

I had lost half of my reproductive organs at such a tender age. I shouldn't have been able to conceive at all. So when I got pregnant with twins and then lost them, I thought that God was punishing me. I thought that God was punishing me for all the mistakes that I had made in my past. I heard all these voices, crazy, screaming brain chatter racing through my mind a million miles a minute, telling me that it was my fault and that I had brought this on myself. Finally, I just surrendered to them and accepted the fact that this was my fate. The cold, hard reality was that I had lost my precious baby boys and what's done is done. I was reaping the fruits that I had sown, and the pain was more than I could bear. I was bleeding to death and I didn't know how to save myself. I was filled with anger and disappointment with God. I thought that He had failed me miserably, both as my father and as my God. I didn't know how to process all the pain that I was experiencing or whether I could ever trust God again. I thought that He was disciplining me, just like He had done so many times to the Israelites in the Bible whenever they sinned against him. Back then, I hadn't experienced God as my Heavenly Father—yet. He was just a Bible character and a very scary one too. My knowledge of God was only in my head—not in my heart. It took a very long time before that revelation of Him had finally reached my heart. My biggest problem was confusing my spiritual father with my earthly father.

As a child growing up, I was afraid of my father. My mother had a psychological belt that went to work every day from 9-5; his name was Dad. Whenever we (meaning my three brothers, two sisters, and I) did something wrong, my mother would just pull out the good ole psychological belt and with just one phrase, "Wait until your father gets home," was all we needed to hear. Those words would drive the fear of God straight through our little hearts like a dagger. No matter what time of the day she would use those words, we would suddenly become extremely tired and went straight to bed. My father rarely spanked us. He had this cold look in his eyes and a chill in his voice that was very frightening to us. He didn't need to physically discipline us. We were afraid of him. That's how I saw God. I saw him as a strict disciplinarian just like my earthly father. Because of that, I spent most of my life fearing Him rather than trusting Him. My concept of God was more like a judge with a huge gavel in his hand just waiting for me to make a mistake so that He can pass down my sentence. It was difficult for me to embrace a God that would allow unspeakable things to happen to good people, especially His children. I was taught that good things happen to good people and bad things happen to bad people. I believe that it is what we call karma nowadays. "You reap what you sow." But I was wrong!

God is nothing like my earthly father. He is nothing at all like I had imagined. All those wasted years I spent running away from the big, mean, scary guy upstairs who says that He's my father, but as soon as I mess up, here comes the belt! It was a lie! A lie from the devil and I bought into it hook, line, and sinker. It took me what almost felt like a lifetime to finally see what the devil was doing to me, and it hurts me to think that I gave him the power to control and manipulate my entire life. Although I knew the teachings of the Bible and I was very good at quoting the scriptures, I really didn't know God at all! I didn't have a personal relationship with him like I thought I had. It was only after God had opened my eyes to the truth and showed me that Satan is a liar and he is the one that comes to kill, steal, and to destroy our lives. Before I came to realize that, I was blaming the wrong person for everything that had gone wrong in my life. I blamed God for everything! It wasn't God that took my babies away from me any more than it was God who wanted me to atone for my sins. God sent his son, Jesus Christ, to atone for my sins so that I wouldn't have to.

From Bad to Worse

Have you ever been in a bad situation and think that it could never possibly get any worse, only to find out that it can? I have, many times. Let's face it, we all have. This is a typical example of what my mother use to say, "Girl, you're getting from bad to worse!" You would think that getting pregnant at seventeen and almost dying—and then finding out that I may never have children—would be enough of a learning experience for me, but it wasn't! I just had to give my parents more gray hairs than I already had. I was the kind of kid that as soon as I was past one crisis, I would run head on into another one. I never even gave myself a chance to breathe before I found myself into another pickle. This time, my face ran into my boyfriend's fist.

When I was eighteen years old, I went to a club one night with a couple of friends and met this man. We hit it off right away. We struck up a conversation, danced, and hung out together most of the night into the wee hours of the morning. We were two of the last people there when the club was closing. During the course of the night, we exchanged telephone numbers, and eventually, we started dating. We dated for about a year before I ended the relationship and had him incarcerated for assault. We were living in two different cities at the time we met—and neither one of us had a car in those days. This was in 1978. I didn't even have a driver's license much less a car. Back then, women weren't as independent as they are today. I would take the bus an hour and a half away from my home to visit this man in Toronto, where he lived. He was quite a bit older than I was, but it didn't matter because I really liked him.

He was a very handsome man, in a roguish sort of a way, and to top that, he was a very good cook. Unlike my husband, I was very attracted to him right off the bat, but most often, pretty looks can be deceiving. And it certainly was in this case. This man was crazy jealous and had a bad temper. He was a control freak! Why can't we see these things before we get into a relationship with morons like this guy? They all seem so normal in the beginning. Then one day we wake up and we're in bed with the devil. This man would fly off the handle if any man looked at me even crossed-eyed. It's perfectly all right that he found me attractive, but God forbid if any other man did too.

By the time he slapped me across the face one night during an argument, we had been dating for several months. I never saw it coming! Yes, I knew he was jealous, but I didn't know that he would actually hit me. Because I lived so far away, I didn't know what to do when he beat me up that night. He was sitting in the living room of his apartment watching television, and I was crying in the bedroom with my face all black and blue. I sat on the edge of the bed, trying to figure out how in the world I was going to get away from this monster. I knew I had to leave, but it was late at night, and I was in another city that I wasn't familiar with. In those days, we didn't have cell phones, and the only phone in the house just happened to be in the living room where he was sitting.

I made a decision to make a run for it—no matter what! I wasn't sure if he was finished beating me up or just taking a ringside break before he started round 2, and I wasn't about to wait around to find out. I was in my pajamas and house slippers, so I had to change my clothes quietly, but I couldn't change my slippers because my shoes were at the front door. Shoes or house slippers, I was leaving! I grabbed my purse and ran straight out the front door before he realized what was happening. I ran down the stairs, and he chased me, but I got away. I flagged down a taxi, jumped into it, and told the driver to drive because my boyfriend was trying to kill me. At that point, I didn't have a plan. My only agenda was to get as far away from this lunatic as I could. Then I remembered that I had an uncle that lived in another city about thirty kilometers away. I couldn't even remember exactly where he lived. I had to ask the taxi driver to stop and let me use a pay phone to call my uncle to get the address. Unfortunately, my uncle wasn't home, but I spoke to my aunt, and she gave me the address.

When I arrived at my uncle's house, I had no money. I had to give the taxi driver my watch to hold in lieu of payment and ask him to come back the next day when my uncle was home to pay him. I think after he saw how bruised my face was and knew that I was trying to get away from a psychopath, he was moved with compassion and agreed to hold my watch and come back the next day for his money. Late that night, after my uncle came home, I could hear him screaming on top of his voice about how he was going to find this man and break both of his legs. He was furious! I pretended to be asleep so that I wouldn't have to face my uncle that night. I felt ashamed for putting myself into such a predicament in the first place. I should have known better.

I said that because I saw the handwriting on the wall many times before that night, but I chose to ignored them. His bad temper and jealousy was a dead giveaway. I knew in my heart that he wasn't the one for me long before he laid a finger on me. There's something that all women should know about men like that. They can talk themselves out of anything. They are professional liars and master mind manipulators. It doesn't matter how many times they apologizes and swear on their mother's grave that they won't hit you again. They will! They can't help it! They're addicted to violence. They feed off your fears, and their ability to control you gives them a high—like a drug. It makes them feel strong to make you feel weak! It's a weapon that they will use repeatedly until someone dies.

I didn't want to die, and I didn't want to become somebody's punching bag either—so I fled. But I wish that I could tell you that it ended that night because it didn't. My uncle and my brother drove me back to his apartment the next day to get my belongings, and I went home vowing that I wouldn't return. A couple of days after I had returned home, he showed up in the city where I lived. He knew fully well that he couldn't show his face at my front door because my father and two brothers would have broken every bone in his pathetic body. So he called me from a pay phone down the street from my house. I answered the telephone—not knowing who it was. In those days, we didn't have caller ID like we have today. He pleaded with me about how remorseful he was and swore that it would never happen again. Women, beware! It's a lie from the pit of hell. Nine out of ten times, they will do it again and again . . .

Any kind of abuse just doesn't happen once. It's an addition—like cocaine. You don't just get up one day and change. Any kind of change takes time and perseverance. It doesn't happen overnight—even if you want to change. I fell for his "I love you and I'm sorry, and I will never hurt you again" sob story. He played me like a Spanish guitar, and I fell right back into his snare. A few weeks later, I was back on the bus to Toronto to see him again. He played nice with me for a while—I'll give him that. He even proposed marriage and bought a ring. That's how far some of these people are willing to go. He was on his best behavior for a couple months, until we had another disagreement; then all that suppressed anger started to raise its ugly head. I could see it coming. I recognized the look in his eyes.

This time, I was a little more prepared. I tried to diffuse the situation by telling him whatever I knew he wanted to hear. This time, I wasn't going to allow him to victimize me again. I played along with him and pretended as if it was just a misunderstanding and everything was good between us. But as soon as he went to the bathroom, I picked up the telephone and called the police. Then I went back into the bedroom, packed up my little weekend bag, and waited for the fireworks. In his mind, we had resolved the issue, and everything was fine, but in my mind, I needed to get away from this maniac and this time for good. I heard when he came out of the bathroom and went back into the living room to watch television. I hid my bag under the bed, sat on the bed, and waited for the knock at the door.

Show time! The knock on the door that could possibly save my life finally came. You could see my heart pounding in my chest through my blouse as I walked out of the bedroom and into the front room just in time to see him opening the door. Two uniformed police officers were standing in the doorway. One of the officers said, "Good afternoon, sir, did someone call from this address for help? My boyfriend said, "No, officer, not from here." I was in the background shaking like a leaf in the wind but doing my best not to show it. I stepped forward a bit and said, "I called, officer. I want to leave, but this man won't let me." As soon as he heard what I said, he lunged at me and started punching me.

The two officers charged at him like linebackers and tried to get him off me. He fought them both fiercely—punching, kicking, and growling at the two policemen. I ran into a corner of the room and crouched into a little ball to protect myself. Hands and feet were flying faster than three drunks in a bar brawl as the two officers wrestled him to the floor trying to restrain him, but he was much too strong for them to pin him down. He managed to break free and fled the scene. One of the police officers called for backup while the other chased after him. The officer checked to see if I was hurt, and I was. I took a lot of blows to my face, but I wasn't hurt bad enough to go to the hospital. The officer asks me where I lived and how I had planned on getting back to Kitchener, which was an hour and a half away.

He instructed me to go into the bedroom and collect my things and then offered to drive me to the bus terminal. I heard him communicating with someone on the radio when I went to get my bag, and by then, more officers were dispatched combing the neighborhood to find this guy. They ultimately apprehended him, and he was arrested and subsequently charged with assault—not just on me but on the two policemen. They had asked me if I wanted to press charges against him for assault, and I said yes. I was asked to testify as a witness for the assault on the two policemen, and I also agreed. I remember, to this day, something that the officer said to me in the squad car on the way to the bus station.

The officer said, "You seem to be a nice young lady. What in the world are you doing with such a loser? I want you to go home and never come back, you hear me?" I gave him my word that I would go home and never return, and I didn't, except for the trial. There was a restraining order against him so that he couldn't contact me or see me at all. So he asked his mother to call me on his behalf and try to convince me to drop the charges against him. As much as I really liked and respected his mother, she was a good Christian woman, I was determined to see him prosecuted for assaulting me. I went back to Toronto for his trial, and I testified against him. I also testified as an independent witness for the two police officers that he also assaulted. He was found guilty and was incarcerated. That was the last time I ever saw him.

That was a very painful lesson, and I say that literally. I learned the hard way about relationships and love at such a tender age. You can't abuse and devastate someone whom you claim to love—that's illogical! This man who claimed to have loved me and asked me to marry him beat me black and blue. To the point where I had to run out of his house, in the middle of the night, in my bed slippers, and use my watch to hold as payment for a taxi fare just to get away from him. That's not love. I don't care how many times he apologized. My brother, Anthony, always said, "Love isn't love until you give it away." In other words, talk is cheap, prove it! You prove it by cherishing and respecting the ones who love. Not by raising your hand or foot to inflict pain by beating them to a pulp—then turn around and tell them how much you love them. That's lunacy! If you are in a relationship like that, with or without children, get out! And don't be afraid to press charges against that person either—even if the abuser is your husband.

Pray and ask God for wisdom, guidance, and protection about your situation. He will tell you what to do and show you how to get out safely, just like He did for me. Can you imagine what would have happened to my life if I had married that man? I would probably be dead. I have seen women and men, with and without children, stay in abusive relationships for all kinds of reasons. When we think about domestic violence, we naturally think that the men are the abusers and the women are the victims—that's not always the case. In a lot of these cases, men are being victimized by their partners too. Abusers, whether men or women, are predators; they thrive on power and control. They want to control everything in the relationship—especially you!

I knew a man that was being abused by his wife for many years. Everyone that knew them saw it and wondered why this man was allowing his wife to dominate and control him. His wife would openly embarrass, belittle, and swear at him in public, and he wouldn't say a word. He never retaliated. One day, out of the blue, he just packed up his things and left. I'm sure it wasn't an overnight decision for him. He had to have planned a way of escape for a while before he finally executed it. After he left, everyone that knew them sympathized with him—not his wife. She was clearly the villain.

If you're in a similar situation like that man was and you want out but you're afraid to start over from scratch, please allow me to offer you a piece of advice—get out! I know another man who is being abused by his wife, but he much rather put up with his wife's bad behavior than to divorce. He's afraid that she's going to take him to the cleaners—financial. All he thinks about is the money while his marriage is sucking the life out of him.

His wife runs a tight ship, and he's on a short leash, and he hates it. But the thought of him starting all over from scratch with no money is paralyzing him. I am glad that even at the tender age of eighteen years old I had the good sense of not hooking my wagon to a falling star. I made a lot of mistakes in my life, but walking away from this man wasn't one of them. God had a plan for my life, and marrying this man wasn't a part of it.

There are some things in life that, unfortunately, we don't have any control over—like the death of my twins. But the things that we do have control over and we can change, we owe it to ourselves to do something about it.

The Perfect Setup

I don't know what happened on that dreadful day when my twins died, but I firmly believe that everything, good and bad, happens for a reason. Although God wasn't responsible for the death of my babies, I knew that He was in control of everything, even their premature death. I came to realize that I was no different than Naomi. The same God that was in control of Naomi's life, the one that had allowed all those tragedies to befall her, was the same God that had allowed my children to die. But just like God had a plan for Naomi's life, He also had one for mine. Sometimes when we suffer a tremendous loss, like the death of a loved one, it's hard for us to believe that all that pain and suffering could possibly work together for our good. That belief was something that I fought fiercely for a very long time.

It seemed cruel and inhumane to think that God would allow the death of my unborn children to be a part of his perfect will for my life. But just like He had allowed Naomi's husband and two sons to die and that was a part of his perfect will for her life, then who am I to question the will of God? God used the famine in Bethlehem to relocate Naomi and her family to Moab, knowing that one of Naomi's sons would meet and marry a Moabites woman named, Ruth. He also knew that Ruth would accompany her mother-in-law back to Bethlehem after the sudden death of her husband and two sons. God used something like the cruel and painful death of Naomi's entire family to position her in the lineage of Jesus Christ.

God had already chosen Ruth, the Moabites, to be one of the vessels that our Lord and Savior Jesus Christ would come through. All along, God was working out his plans for Naomi's life, but she didn't know it. She thought that God had forsaken her, even testified against her, and can you blame her for thinking that? I would. And I think that most of us would too. All she had experienced up to that point were losses: the loss of her home when she had to move from Bethlehem-Judah to Moab (an idol-worshipping country) and the loss of her husband and two sons who died suddenly and left her with two daughter-in-laws that she couldn't afford to take care of.

She must have felt totally lost and confused. This woman was certainly no stranger to losses. If anyone had a good reason to get bitter with God, it was definitely Naomi. She actually said that God had testified against her, but what she didn't know was that her testimony was about to change. Sometimes, we go through seasons in our lives where we feel like God has forsaken us, even afflicted us, like Naomi. But God promised us that He would never leave us nor forsake us even unto the end of the world. The apostle Paul wrote in Second Corinthians 4:17, "For our light affliction, which is but for a moment, is working for us a far more exceeding and eternal weight of glory." The "light afflictions" that Paul was talking about were being beaten, blinded, shipwrecked, hunger, sickness, and at times homelessness; try putting that on for size and see how you would handle it. I'm sure it would be a tad bit overwhelming.

But the mistake that Naomi made was the same mistake that I made. We were both focusing on all the losses in our lives. Our eyes were on the death of our loved ones rather than where God was taking us. Naomi was so consumed with the grief of losing her entire family and rightly so, but her life wasn't over—only one chapter. She didn't realize how much more living and dreaming she had left. She had her eyes fixed on all the closed doors, lost opportunities, and disappointments that she couldn't see the endless possibilities that she possessed in Ruth.

Her daughter-in-law, Ruth, was the key to her salvation. Ruth was Naomi's RRSP, her old-age security and her retirement fund all rolled up in one. Can you imagine someone loving you so much that they would leave their own country and abandon their family, even their religion for you? Well, that's what Ruth did! She wasn't tied to Naomi anymore. Her husband was dead, and she had no children. She could have easily just picked up and gone anywhere. But because she loved her mother-in-law so much and wanted to be with her, she left her entire life behind to follow this old woman. God had a plan, and it was He who knitted these two women's hearts together.

God's plan was bigger than what they both could have ever imagined. Exceeding, abundantly, above all that they could think or ask. That's how much God loved them, and that's how God shows His love for His children. Ruth was Naomi's living legacy. She was God's reward to Naomi for her faithfulness to Him. And because of Ruth, Naomi was privileged to be positioned in the lineage of Jesus Christ. What an honor! Naomi had no idea that God had highly favored her and that her retirement was going to be spent in ease.

All along, God was setting her up for a blessing, and everything that she had to go through were all stepping stones to something far greater than she could have ever dreamed. If we're able to look past the disappointments and failures in our past and trust God with our future, we'll see that He is doing the same thing for us that He did for Naomi. He's getting us ready for a blessing, and all the difficulties that we go through are all a part of His plans to get us to our final destination. God is not trying to hurt us; neither has He forgotten us. He's just trying to set us up for a blessing.

CHAPTER 2

Don't Get Bitter Because of the Process

You Can't Hide from Your Problems

In the past, whenever I was going through a deep emotional crisis, I always had a proclivity to run away. I mean, I would actually get on an airplane and just fly off somewhere. It didn't matter too much to me where the airplane was headed just as long as I was on it. I would tell myself that if I put enough distance between me and the problem, the problem would go away. Imagine that! Talk about being ridiculous! I remember one time, I ran off to Cuba for a week just because I was going through a difficult time. I would tell my husband that I needed a little time alone to figure things out, which is another way of saying, "I've got to get out of here. I can't do this."

I must have used that excuse a million times during the course of my marriage. But if the truth be known, I really didn't need time to think. I needed somewhere to hide. I needed some place far away from my problems so that I wouldn't have to focus on them. Early in my marriage, my husband tried to reason with me about my foolish escapades and how they were affecting our marriage, but I wouldn't listen. Countless times, he tried to explain to me how rejected he felt every time I ran off on one of my whims, but I couldn't stop. He interpreted my need to get away, especially without him, as an act of abandonment. He felt shut out of the marriage. My little disappearing acts were slowly eroding my marriage, but I was completely oblivious to it.

Years later, when I asked my husband why he didn't divorce me, he told me that marriage is for better and for worse, and those years epitomized the "for worse" in our marriage. I carried that guilt and shame for a long time, knowing that I had put such a good and decent man through all that heartache and pain. I thank God every day that he gave me a husband that actually believes and still upholds every word of the vows that he made to me two times in one lifetime. Did I mention that I married my husband twice? I will talk about it a little later on in the book. Running away from our problems is never an option! It only prolongs the inevitable! Problems are designed by God to draw us closer to Him. And as we draw closer to Him, He works out his will and purpose in our lives. Disappointments and hurts are not intended to drive a wedge between us and God. As a matter of fact, it's the opposite. They are intended to encourage us to seek after the problem solver.

Greatness Has a Price Tag

Look at Joseph (Gen. 37); he experienced more than his share of setbacks, and some, but he never allowed himself to get bitter because of the process. Joseph's problems started when he was just a lad. When other boys his age were playing cops and robbers in their backyards with their brothers, Joseph was dodging real bullets from his brothers! Children are supposed to be carefree and full of hopes and dreams, but not Joseph. He started having problems at a much tender age than he should have. Jacob, Joseph's father, had twelve sons, each of them special and unique in their own way. But Jacob loved Joseph more than all his children because he was the child of his old age and because of who his mother was. Rachel, Joseph's mother, was the love of Jacob's life, but she died, prematurely, shortly after giving birth to their second son, Benjamin. Joseph's brothers, all but Benjamin, hated him because he was their father's favorite. But after Joseph foolishly told them about a dream that he had, where they all bowed down to him, they hated him even more. More so, that they wanted him dead!

Sometimes when God speaks to us about our future, we have to be careful who we tell! That's exactly what happened to Joseph. He shared his dream with his brothers, thinking that it was safe to trust them. But instead, they were filled with envy and plotted to kill him. It was only after Simeon, one of the brothers, warned the others not to kill their own brother but to sell him into slavery instead they decided not to kill Joseph. The evil brothers devised a plan to sell their baby brother into slavery and tell their father that he was killed by a wild animal.

Joseph was their baby brother! They were supposed to protect him and set good examples for him to follow, like older brothers ought to do. Instead, they were too busy orchestrating a plan to get rid of their brother and lie to their poor old father. Whatever would possess Joseph to confide in his brothers? He knew that they didn't like him! He knew that they were jealous of him! If Joseph hadn't told them about his dream, they wouldn't have sold him into slavery. But maybe, it was all a part of God's plan for Joseph's life. You must be thinking right now, "My god, what kind of a god would allow one of His children to be sold into slavery as a part of His plan for their life?" The kind of God that can see how the story is going to end and that the end result possesses a glorious purpose. If God didn't know that, He would have disarmed the plan rather than allowing it.

Some pain is caused or permitted by God for a greater purpose. And in this case, God knew Joseph's limit. He knew exactly how much suffering he could take without destroying him. It might have taken over thirteen years for Joseph's dreams to come to pass, but he never gave up. He never gave up dreaming, and neither should you! When God gives you a dream or a promise, nothing can stop it from coming to pass but you. You're the only one that can sabotage what God is doing in your life. You can stop or delay God's plans for your life by trying to manipulate the outcome. If you are guilty of doing that, stop it immediately! Step back and trust God's way of doing things. What God is looking for in all of us is exactly what He saw in Joseph, faith! God saw something special in him—his heart. God saw a heart that was full of faith. And God knew that no matter what process He had to put Joseph through, he wouldn't get bitter. God is looking for people that won't quit or get bitter because of the process. We all have to go through something in order to get something and that stage is called "process."

I grew up thinking that salvation was free. But now, I have come to realize that nothing is for free, not even salvation. Our salvation may not have cost us anything. It's a gift. But the price of salvation is costly. It cost God something. It cost Him His only begotten son, and it cost Jesus Christ His life. God forbid if we have to suffer a while or go through trials in order to achieve greatness. Greatness has a price, and sometimes, it comes after much suffering. We all want to be rich or, at the very least, financially stable. But success has a price. It's called hard work.

Unfortunately, most of us don't want to work for a living. We want God to hand success to us on a silver platter. Some of us want to win the lottery or we want God to rain down hundred dollar bills from heaven upon us—I wouldn't mind that at all. Then, there are those who want that promotion at work but are unwilling to go in early and stay late in order to get it. It's much easier to kiss up to the boss or do a little backstabbing once in a while in order to get ahead. Sometimes God has to take us through a process. He does this in order to prepare us for the task at hand. He has to make sure that when the time comes, we will be ready.

The Heart of God

Before God chooses us for greatness, He first looks at our heart above all. He knows the ones that won't get bitter like Joseph. Joseph, out of all the twelve sons of Jacob, had the kind of heart that God was looking for. He had a heart that would forgive his brothers even after they had betrayed him and sold him into slavery. He had a heart that trusted God no matter what! He had a heart that trusted God even after God had allowed him to go to prison for a crime that he didn't commit. He had a heart that continually praised God even in the midst of his sufferings. Joseph had a heart that wouldn't give up on God no matter what!

Joseph was fully persuaded that one day, God would deliver him and recompense him for all his troubles. Most of us, unlike Joseph, would be sitting in prison plotting and scheming about how to take revenge on our enemies. And with each passing day, we would become bitter and cold against everyone, even against God. If only we were more like Joseph and less like his brothers whose hearts were filled with jealousy and hate. Joseph's brothers were always jealous of him, not just because he was their father's favorite, but because they too saw something great in him and they coveted it.

When you have a heart after God's heart, it will separate you from the rest and others will see it. Some may even hate you for it, even in your own family. Can you imagine how Joseph must have felt? Just put yourself into his shoes for a minute. How would you feel if your own family hated you? Yet he remained faithful to God in everything that he did. And as a result, God blessed the work of Joseph's hands even while he was going through hell. God gave Joseph favor in everything! With Potiphar, his slave master, when he served in his house. With the jailer while he was in prison. That's the beauty of the Lord; He will cause you to prosper even in the midst of adversity. That's the reason why Joseph named his first son Manasseh, meaning, "For God has made me forget all my toil and all my father's house." And he called the name of his second son Ephraim, meaning, "For God has caused me to be fruitful in the land of my affliction." Do you know that God can bless you even in prison? He blessed Joseph, didn't he? All along, God was setting him up for a blessing.

Are you incarcerated and feel like you're never going to get out of prison? Maybe that's how Joseph felt while he was imprisoned. He was just an innocent boy that was victimized by his own brothers. It doesn't matter if you're innocent or guilty of the crime for which you are incarcerated; your life isn't over, and God still has a plan in mind for you. God sees our mistakes long before they happen, but He doesn't love us because we are good. If that was the case, none of us could ever be good enough to earn God's love. God loves us because He is good. Only God can take our mistakes and turn it around for good. Only God can give us beauty for ashes. God can use us wherever we are even if we're in prison.

The thought of never living a normal life again might seem impossible to you right now, but God wants to do the impossible in your life, but only if you really want Him to. You might just find the next time you come up for parole, even if you've been denied several times already; it could very well be your day for a miracle. Suddenly, God could show up in your circumstances and change your life forever. Why not? It happened to me, and it could happen for you too.

The Cult

There was a time in my life when I didn't believe that God still worked miracles, until I found myself needing one. By then, I didn't have anything more to lose, except my pride. I too made a lot of mistakes in my life, and one of my many mistakes landed me in jail. I remember crying out loud one night, "God! If you can hear me and you still perform miracles, I need one right now!" I was a nineteen-year-old high school dropout who didn't have a clue who I was or what I wanted to do with the rest of my life. At that time, I was still living at home with my parents, doing everything that teenagers do to make their parents lives a living hell. I didn't just get up one day and decide to make it my number 1 priority to destroy my parents' lives, but I almost succeeded.

I had just gone through what I thought was the worst thing that could ever happen to me, but what I was about to face made my past mistakes seem like a walk in the park. I still don't know to this day what was wrong with me, but I thank God that I had parents who loved me. My parents were good, hardworking people. And although I was raised in a middle class home with three brothers and two sisters, I was like a huge magnet that only attracted bad things and bad people. More often than I care to admit, I found myself in and out of trouble all the time. I was always getting involved with the wrong people who were doing the wrong things, but when I got involved with a group of people who called themselves Rastafarians that was the straw that broke the camel's back.

The Rastafarians believed and practiced a lot of things, but one of the things that I truly admired the most was the simplicity of their lifestyle. They were simple, back-to-nature kind of people, and you could see it in the way they dressed and how they lived, but they were totally against Christianity and the teachings about the deity of Jesus Christ. They believed that the emperor Haile Selassie of Ethiopia was the true messiah and not Jesus Christ as Christianity teaches. Although their lifestyle totally contradicted everything I was taught and believed, for example, their frequent use of marijuana, their common-law multiple-partners relationships, and a lot more, I just couldn't stop hanging around them. It was like an addiction.

The more time I spent with them, the more I wanted to be around them. And before I realized what was happening, I found myself rejecting my Christian roots and embracing theirs. I stopped combing my hair and started matting it. The matting of the hair was considered to be one of the outward symbols of a true Rastafarian. But what I didn't know at the time was that there is nothing authentic about a cult, and in my opinion, that is what Rastafari is. Their beliefs and idealisms were similar to that of Jim Jones, also called the Mad Messiah, in the Guyana massacre back in 1978. I foolishly joined the Rastafarians in their futile efforts of creating an imaginable utopia that ultimately led to one of the worst mistakes of my entire life. I abandoned my Christian beliefs and started doing things that I had never done before. Dreadful things, like getting arrested for drugs when I had never even smoked a cigarette a day in my entire life.

I was arrested at the airport with a suitcase filled with marijuana and was subsequently charged with possession of a narcotic for the purpose of trafficking. As rebellious as I was in those days, the one thing that I never did was drugs! I made a promise to myself, when I was a little girl growing up in Jamaica and saw firsthand how smoking cigarettes almost killed my father that I would never smoke or do any kind of drugs, and I never broke that promise— ever! But there I was, at nineteen years old, being hauled away in handcuffs like a common criminal for getting involved in a cult!

My first night in jail was a nightmare! I remember lying on a dirty lumpy cot in a holding cell behind the airport and said to myself, "Althea, what kind of a mess did you get yourself into this time?" I stayed awake all night, crying and pleading with God to help me. I never felt more anxious and alone than I did that night! The little girl in me was screaming out for her daddy's arms to hold her and comfort her, but what I didn't realized was that God, my Heavenly Father, was right there in the jail cell with me. Thoughts of my parents and what they were going through kept racing through my mind. The news of their teenage daughter being arrested and thrown into jail for drugs must have been overwhelming for them, to say the least.

Fortunately, my father was out of the country at the time of my arrest. But my dear old mother, she must have been beside herself. I felt so ashamed and disappointed in myself for putting my parents through all that embarrassment—something that they definitely did not deserve. They were good parents, especially my mother. My father was different, which I will talk more about later on in the book, but nevertheless, I let them down in the worst possible way. Immediately after my father learned of my arrest, he took the first flight home. He was trying desperately to get home in time for my bail hearing, which was in two days. As much as I dreaded the thought of facing a judge in court, I think that I was even more afraid of seeing the look of disappointment on my parents' faces. That's something that I never want to see again for the rest of my life. They had to put up our house as security for my release. My parents hired an expensive attorney that came highly recommended as a shark. This attorney was infamous for representing drug dealers and gang members, and his fee reflected his reputation. But my parents were determined to keep me out of prison no matter the cost.

The Prison Guard

I spent five days in jail before I was finally released on bail. During those five days, I experienced the favor of the Lord unlike anything I had ever experienced before, starting with the night at the airport when I was arrested and charged with possession of a narcotic for the purpose of trafficking rather than importing a narcotic for the purpose of trafficking. Apparently, a possession charge is a lesser charge than importing, and if convicted, it carries a lighter sentence. I didn't know this until the judge, at my bail hearing, questioned the arresting officer as to why he only charged me with possession rather than importing.

The favor of the Lord was already at work at day 1 by putting all the right people across my path every step of the way, just like He did for Joseph. Remember how God gave Joseph favor with the jailer? Well, He did the same thing for me too. God gave me favor with one of the prison guards at the holding center where I was incarcerated. This was my first time behind bars, and after just one night, I made a promise to myself that it would be my last. Prison life was nothing like what I had seen on television. It was not scripted, and I wasn't an actress playing a role as an inmate. It was real, and if convicted, I was looking at seven years behind bars.

I was only nineteen years old, and I was still living at home when this happened. I saw things that I wished I hadn't seen. In those days, I didn't have a clue what homosexuality was and the word "gay" meant happy. I just about had a heart attack when I saw women kissing and doing things that I thought only men and women did. I just had to get out of there. I was confused! I thought that I was hallucinating. And my cell was almost the size of the closet in my bedroom at home, except for the little toilet in a corner of the room. I cried day and night for five days straight. I couldn't eat, I couldn't sleep, I kept to myself all the time, and I hardly said a word except for when I was spoken to. I was petrified! If it hadn't been for the nice prison guard that kept encouraging me to eat, I probably would have starved to death. He noticed that I wasn't eating and became concerned about my health. He was a kind compassionate man that just took a liking to me and went out of his way to help me in whatever way he could.

After three days of hardly eating anything, he struck a deal with me to get me to eat. He told me that if I ate supper that night, he would call my parents on the telephone, allow me to talk to them for a little bit. That was all I needed to hear, and suddenly, I got my appetite back. I ate everything that was on my dinner tray, and he kept his word. He took me into one of the offices and called my parents and handed me the telephone. As soon as I heard my mother's voice, I just broke down and started to cry. Her tender words of love and comfort kept me together along with my new prison guard friend that had become my guardian angel sent by God to watch over me.

For the remainder of the time that I was there, he faithfully watched over me just to make sure that I ate and that I was safe. I saw the heart of God in that prison guard and it reassured me that God was right there in prison with me. God knows what we need when we need it, and He promised us that He would never leave us or forsake us. There are so many blessings that we take for granted every day without ever giving a thought to them. But when I walked out of that jail after being locked up with a bunch of strangers, I realized for the first time how fortunate I truly was to have a Heavenly Father watching over me all the time.

By the time I got home to the little provincial town that I was living in, the news of my arrest had become the topic at everyone's dinner table. Our family was very well known in the community for being a good Christian family, so you can just imagine the shock when the rumors started circulating about how my father gave me drugs to carry back from Jamaica for him. It seemed as if everyone that was talking about me had put their own spin on the story just to make things a bit more interesting. When you live in a small boring city like the one that I grew up in, the weather report is usually the topic of the day. The news of my arrest was probably the biggest newsflash to hit that city in a very long time, so I must have wagged a few tongues to say the very least.

I remember how long it took me to show my face in public for the first time. I was too ashamed to face anyone I knew, especially friends. I had to ask my brother, Anthony, to drive me to my appointments, including my weekly appointments at the local correctional center. It was a part of my bail agreement to report there once a week pending trial. I did that faithfully for three years because that's how long it took before my case went to trial. It was probably the worst three years of my entire life, and I never would have survived the entire ordeal if it hadn't been for my family. Some of my friends, the so-called ones, had abandoned me, and the gossiping was outrageous.

It's usually during the hard times when you need your friends the most. And it's also in the hard times you find out who your friends really are. I felt so alone and ostracized that I actually thought about running away from my family and from prosecution every waking hour of the day. I couldn't bear the thought of going to prison for one day, much less for years. It took all the strength that I had, which was very little, to trust God to get me out of the mess that I was in. If it hadn't been for my brother, Anthony, I probably would have fled prosecution. It was something that he said why I stayed. He told me that if I ran away, I would be on the run for the rest of my life. He made me realize that I would never see my family and feel safe ever again. The thought of looking over my shoulders for the rest of my life was frightening. That was not how I had intended to live my life.

One of the things that I have learned from growing up in the church is that prayer is the same as just talking to God. I learned that I didn't need to use a lot of fancy words or quotes from the Bible in order to speak to God. All I had to do is just speak honestly from my heart like I would if I were talking to a friend. So I did a lot of talking, and I believe that God did a lot of listening because three years later, I was found not guilty. God had heard my prayers, and he gave me back my life. The Bible says in Luke 1:37, "For with God, nothing shall be impossible." I can truly testify to that because if God hadn't intervened, I would have gone to prison for a very long time. So you may be going through a bad time right now and think that there's no way out of your predicament, but that's not true. God is always working behind the scenes on our behalf, and it's never over until God says it's over. Whether your story ends like Joseph's or mine. And by the way, Joseph's story had a happy ending. God gave him favor with Pharaoh, and he was eventually released from prison and was promoted. Joseph became the second most powerful man in all of Egypt next to Pharaoh. He went from a prison cell to the palace halls, and only God could have done that.

The Mystery Judge

Whatever you are going through right now, God is the only one that has the power to turn your situation around. Why don't you ask Him right now, right where you are, to give you back your life. What do you have to lose? Maybe God has the perfect setup arranged for you. Do you want to know how I was found not guilty? I waited three long years for my case to go to trial, and by then, I had met the most wonderful man in the world, which is now my husband of over twenty-seven years. We met in 1980 just about a year after I was arrested on drug charges. So we were only dating for about two years before my case went to trial. I was completely honest and up front with him about the seriousness of the charges against me. I wanted him to know that if I were to be convicted, I was going away to prison for a very long time. I thought for sure that once I made that clear to him, he would run for the hills. I thought to myself, "There's no way this guy is going to wait years for me to come out of prison. After all, I'm not his wife, and even if I were, he still wouldn't wait for me." I thought that I was hearing things when he told me that he would be there for me no matter what. Nobody does that unless they're truly in love.

Finally, the day of the trial came, and all I could think about on my way to the courthouse was the promise that I had made to God on the night that I was arrested. I had promised God that if He kept me out of prison, I would clean up my act and stop hanging around with the wrong people. I meant every word of it, and all I needed was a chance to make good on my promise. The drive to the courthouse was about an hour away from the city where I lived. The silence in the car was deafening. All I could think about was that I might not go home again—not for a very long time.

My brain chatter wouldn't shut up! At that moment, I saw my entire life flashed before my eyes. All the mistakes that I had made and how much I had regretted every one of them. I saw all my hopes and dreams slipping through my fingers like sand and I was afraid. When we arrived at the courthouse, my lawyer was waiting for us in the foyer. As soon as we entered the building, my lawyer told me how nice I looked and then he dropped the bomb on us about the judge that was presiding over my case.

Apparently, the judge that was supposed to try my case suddenly became ill, and a strange judge was assigned to my case. At that point, nobody had ever heard about this particular judge—not even the prosecutor. It seemed that this judge came from out of the province. Both my lawyer and the prosecutor didn't have a clue about his demeanor. I saw the grim look on my lawyer's face as he broke the news to us, but I never fully understood why that was a problem until he explained to us that usually defense lawyers and prosecutors are acquainted with one another and with the judges.

He told us that lawyers have a general idea what to expect during a trial based on the judge that is presiding over the case. Apparently, lawyers know the judges who are a lot more lenient on first-time offenders and the ones who are hard-nosed especially in drug-related offences. In my case, they had no clue who this judge was or whether or not he was tough or lenient on first-time offenders. After hearing all that, I felt my heart exploded inside my chest. I felt like my life was over, and I was going to prison for sure. I felt hopeless! The only thing I knew to do at that time was to pray. And so I prayed for two days straight. That's how long the trial lasted.

Not Guilty!

On the last day of the trial, I was asked to take the stand. Even though my lawyer had prepared me months in advance as what to expect during cross-examination, I still wasn't prepared for what happened in the courtroom that day. I had expected to be questioned thoroughly by the prosecutor, being extra cautious for trick questions and accusations, but I was totally caught off guard when the judge asked to question me after the prosecutor had finished grilling me. If I wasn't sitting down at the time, I probably would have fainted. My heart was beating so fast that I thought that it was going to jump right out of my chest. Suddenly, my mouth became dry, and my tongue cleaved to the roof of my mouth. I certainly wasn't ready for this! I couldn't imagine what in the world he wanted to ask me.

The judge picked up a piece of paper that was in front of him and started reading it. Then he said, "Miss Lee, this is a list of the items that you had in your possession when you were arrested. I see that you had a Bible with you. Why is that?" Of all the questions he could have asked, why would he want to know why I had a Bible in my suitcase? I was puzzled! I wasn't sure if this was the trick question I was anticipating, but it was one of the easiest ones of all since the trial started. I explained to him that I had always carried a Bible with me whenever I travelled. I can still remember the weird look on the judge's face when I said it. And what was even stranger was that he never bothered to ask me why. I believe that it was at that moment the judge made up his mind and returned with a "not guilty" verdict.

That day was the first time I had ever seen my father cry. It wasn't like I didn't know that my father loved me, but it was the first time he took off his tough guy mask and showed his vulnerability. In my opinion, God worked two miracles that day. I left the courthouse feeling elated. I was free! But the most bizarre thing happened while we were getting ready to leave, we saw the judge that had just tried my case walk past us and exit the building. Afterwards, we found out that the judge was only scheduled to try my case alone for those two days. This strange judge that nobody had ever heard of, until the first day of my trial, presided over my case only and then just disappeared afterward. To this day, I am convinced that he was an angel sent by God. Maybe you don't believe in angels or miracles. All I know is that I saw my life slipping away, and I wasn't about to stand back and watch it happen without doing something about it. So I prayed and believed God for a miracle, and I received one. Do you need a miracle? Then, why don't you ask God for one.

Why Me, Lord?

Looking back over the events that led up to that dark and terrible day, the day that my twins died, I still don't understand any of it. I still don't know why God helped me all those other times but not this time. What was so different about this particular situation why God chose to turn a blind eye to it? This was important; at least, I thought it was. It was a matter of life or death, the lives or deaths of two innocent babies. So when I found myself lying in that hospital bed, fighting to hold on to them, I thought for sure that God was going to come through for me again, but He didn't. Was it a setup or a major let down? Perhaps both! All I knew was that I expected the same God that delivered me from going to prison in 1981 to show up on August 4, 1988, in my hospital room and to do it again.

Why did God speak in one particular crisis and remain silent in another? Exactly what did I say to Him the first time that I didn't say that day why He didn't show up and save my babies! Was it because I didn't offer Him something in exchange for the lives of my children why God did nothing? Maybe it wasn't something that I had said but how I said it. Or maybe, sparing the lives my babies weren't as important as me going to prison. I didn't know why then, and I still don't know why now even though it has been over twenty years. In my experience, I find that it's pointless to ask God why about anything. Because more often that we care to admit, He's not going to answer. Let's face it people; it all comes down to the will of God. Nobody knows what's in the mind of God. Isaiah 55:8-9 said, "For My thoughts are not your thoughts, Nor are your ways My ways," says the Lord. "For as the heavens are higher than the earth, so are My ways higher than your ways, and My thoughts than your thoughts."

What Is God Waiting For?

"Therefore the Lord will wait, that He may be gracious to you; And therefore He will be exalted, that He may be gracious to you: for the Lord is a God of judgment: blessed are all they that wait for him," (Isa. 30:18, NKJ).

There are many reasons why God delays answers to our prayers, and it's never because He doesn't love us. And He's not trying to punish us either! I would like to discuss some of the most common reasons why God waits before He answers our prayers. Remember the story about a man called Lazarus? (John 11) Lazarus had two sisters, Mary and Martha, and they were very good friends of Jesus'. Lazarus was such a good friend of Jesus' that whenever Jesus came to his town to minister, He and His disciples would stay at Lazarus's house.

The Bible said that Jesus loved Lazarus. So when Lazarus became ill and was sick unto death, naturally, his two sisters sent news of their brother's illness to Jesus and asked Him to come right away. Although they knew that Jesus would want to know that his dear friend was sick, they also had an ulterior motive. They didn't want their brother to die, and they knew that Jesus had the power to heal him. Mary and Martha were convinced that if Jesus were to get to their brother right away, he would be spared. But strange as it were, when Jesus got the message that his dearest friend was dying, He didn't rush off to be with him at all. Actually, He went about his business as usual and waited purposely until after Lazarus was dead and buried before He went to see him. By then, Martha and Mary were devastated with grief over the death of their beloved brother. As the story goes, it was Martha who went out to meet Jesus when she heard of His arrival.

Can you imagine what must have been going through her mind while she was on her way to meet him? She must have been extremely upset and disappointed in Him for taking so long to come. Wouldn't you? Martha knew that Jesus was the Son of God and that He had power to heal her brother. It was only natural for her to have wondered why He hadn't come sooner, especially since she knew that He had received the news long before her brother died. Jesus was Lazarus's friend, and He loved him. Why then did He intentionally wait until after His friend was dead and buried before He showed up? Jesus waited because He wanted to demonstrate His power by raising Lazarus from the dead. If Jesus had come and prayed for Lazarus while he was sick and he had recovered, it could have been construed as something other than a miracle. You know how people are! They would much rather believe it was just luck or the magic of some ancient Chinese potion than to believe it was a miracle. Jesus wanted to eliminate every doubt. He wanted to make sure that everyone knew that He had power to raise the dead.

What is God waiting for in your life before He shows up? Is He intentionally delaying your miracle until your situation looks dead before He speaks? Maybe you're experiencing a crisis, loss, disappointment, or shattered dreams; whatever you are facing that looks hopeless and dead like Lazarus was, God has a plan! If His plan is to breathe life back into your Lazarus, then that's what He's going to do! Nothing is ever lost or unsalvageable with God. God is not helpless among the ruins of your life. Jesus said in John 11:25, "I am the resurrection and the life: He who believes in Me, though he may die, he may live." Although Jesus was consoling Mary and Martha about the death of their brother, Lazarus, He was also saying that He has the power to resurrect anything or anyone at anytime. But as you and I already know, sometimes, God makes us wait, and in this case, God waited because He wanted to demonstrate His power.

In 1997, I had the privilege of witnessing another demonstration of the power of God like Mary and Martha witnessed with their brother, Lazarus. Although I have never witness something as spectacular as someone coming back from the dead, I saw someone that was blind received his sight. My brother, Mario, had an accident and was blinded in his left eye when he was only four years old. When he was thirty-two years old, he was renovating a house that he had bought . . . his first house, and one of the workmen stepped on a piece of ceramic tile that was lying on the ground, and it shattered. A small piece of tile it flew into his good eye and damaged the cornea. He sought immediate medical attention, but the damaged cornea wasn't diagnosed until sometime later after the eye had became extremely infected. To make a long story short, the doctors in Jamaica—that's where my brother lives—weren't able to help him, so he was referred to an ophthalmologist in Canada.

By the time he travelled to Canada and was examined by a doctor, he had to undergo emergency surgery in order to save his life. His eye was so badly infected that the doctors feared that the infection had seeped into his brain and would potentially kill him. Any hope of saving the eye at that point was gone. His condition was grave, and anything short of a miracle to save his life wouldn't have been enough. It wasn't about saving the eye anymore; it was about saving his life. We prayed without ceasing and asked God to intervene and work a miracle on his behalf. We believed that the same God that raised Lazarus from the dead was more than able, not only to save my brother's eye, but also his life. But after we received the devastating news that the doctors had removed the eye and my brother was completely blind, our faith was shaken and our hearts were broken. My brother had a wife and four small children. All we could think about was how we were going to break the news to him.

Although our faith was shaken and our hearts were broken, we never stopped praying for God to turn the situation around. If ever someone needed a miracle, my brother needed one. For hours after the surgery, our ears were glued to the telephone waiting for news. We all feared how he was going to take the news once he came out of recovery. We anxiously waited for him to open his eyes, but dreading what his reaction would be when he opens his eyes to total darkness. We wondered how he was going to be able to care for his wife and four children now. My brother was blind, and his life, as he knew it, was going to change forever. While we were crying out to God, something extraordinary happened! My brother woke up, and the only eye that he had left, the one that was dead for twenty-eight years, suddenly came back to life, and he was able to see again. God didn't save the infected eye. He chose to restore sight to an eye that had been dead for twenty-eight years. God resurrected my brother's dead eye just like He had resurrected Lazarus from the dead. He deliberately waited until after the surgeon had removed the infected eye, and my brother's condition looked impossible before He worked a miracle.

God Waits Because We're Not Ready Yet!

This is probably the number 1 reason why God delays answering our prayers; it's because we're not ready yet. It's like me buying a real expensive car for my twelve-year-old son Philip but have to put it into storage because he's not ready yet. First of all, he's not old enough, and second, he doesn't have a license that gives him the right to operate a vehicle. He's just not ready yet! That's exactly what happened to the children of Israel on the longest short trip in history. When God called Moses to lead the children of Israel out of Egypt and out of bondage, He never intended for them to wander in the wilderness for forty years. The actual trip was only supposed to be an eleven day journey, but God prolonged the trip because they weren't ready to possess their inheritance.

Their constant murmuring and complaining was proof of their immaturity and lack of faith. Their rebellion tied God's hands from releasing His blessing upon them when He wanted to. God didn't want to withhold anything from them! God is our father, and every good father wants to give good gifts to his children. But it was their total lack of faith in God and His choice in leadership that kept them going around in circles for forty years. They didn't trust God, and if they didn't trust God, they were definitely not going to trust Moses' ability to lead them into the Promise Land. Imagine that! God had such big plans for them, just like He does for us, but we're not ready! In my son Philip's case, he wouldn't be ready to take hold of his gift because of something totally out of his control, unlike the children of Israel. It's not my son's fault that he's only twelve years old and cannot legally operate a vehicle. But on the other hand, the children of Israel chose to harden their hearts and rebelled against God by rebelling against Moses. It was clearly their choice!

More often than we care to admit, we miss our blessings or delay our breakthrough because we don't possess the kind of faith in God that produces results. When God gives us a promise, He is giving us His word. God is not like us. He is not a man that He should lie. God wants to give us the desires of our hearts. He wants to make our dreams come true, but He can't! God can't because without faith it is impossible to please Him. So He has to allow us to wander around in our own tailor-made wilderness in order to starve our flesh and build our faith. Although this process is brutally painful, it works! It will yield much fruits and speed up the waiting time during each contraction. We've got to put reasoning and trying to figure out what God is doing out of our minds and just trust His plans and directions for our lives.

I can just hear what some of you are saying right now, "Are you for real? Do you have any idea how hard that is?" Yes, I do! I know how hard it was for me to trust God through every difficult circumstance in my life. Trusting God was something that I had to learn, and believe me when I say that I learned it the hard way. But it was during those difficult times that I learned the most valuable lessons. And as strange as this may sound, I wouldn't trade one ounce of the suffering for nothing. It was through my greatest and darkest wilderness experiences that I saw the power of God demonstrated in a greater way in my life. It was when I felt the weakest and the most vulnerable that God's strength was made perfect in my weakness.

I remember a time when I was going through a real dark period in my life; I was so depressed and heartbroken that I wanted to die. I felt like I had fallen into a pit, and I couldn't come out. Then one night, I had a dream. It was that dream that God used to confirm the writing of this book. If you have been waiting on God to do something in your life for a very long time but nothing is happening, maybe you're tying God's hands and delaying your own miracle by not trusting God to work things out in His way.

God Waits Because He Has an Appointed Time

Earlier, I talked about God intentionally delaying answers to prayers, whether to demonstrate his power like He did with Lazarus and my brother or to do a work in our hearts like He's doing in my heart. No matter what the reasons are, God is always doing something even when He appears to be silent. Although there are numerous reasons for delayed answers to prayers, there is one more that I would like to share with you in this chapter. Seasons! God is a god of seasons, and He's faithful to seasons. "To everything there is a season, a time for every purpose under heaven: A time to be born, and a time to die, a time to plant, and a time to pluck up that is planted" (Eccl. 3:1-2, NKJ).

God operates in what we call seasons, and He does so in the same way the earth has four seasons. Just like the farmer has a time to sow and a time to reap what he has sown (harvest), so it is with God, and He is always faithful to that process. Sometimes when God delays an answer to prayer, it's because it's not harvest time as yet. You might spend your entire life doing the right things and being good to everyone else but yourself, only to watch the same people that you have helped reject you and forget about you. But God has not forgotten you; He has your name engraved upon the palms of his hands (Isa. 49:15-16). Your harvest is coming. God is faithful to the law of sowing and reaping.

The story of Abraham and his wife, Sarah, in Genesis chapter 18 is a good example of seasons. God gave Abraham a promise of a son by his wife, Sarah, but many years had passed and she bore him no children. Years later, after Sarah had passed the age of child bearing, God reassured them in Genesis 18:14, saying, "Is anything too hard for the Lord? At the appointed time, I will return to you, according to the time of life, and Sarah shall have a son." I'm sure that Sarah and her husband must have wondered why God was taking so long to give them children. I would! After all, He had already told them that He was going to give them a son. But what He didn't tell them was when. All God told them was that He had an appointed time.

Long before God gave Abraham the promise of a son, He had already predestined the very day, hour, and even the minute that Sarah, his wife, would conceive and give birth to Isaac. God did not delay answering their prayers because of their lack of faith; on the contrary, God said that Abraham believed Him, and it was counted unto him for righteousness. It means that Abraham believed God immediately after He said it, but God waited on purpose. He waited for one reason and one reason only. It wasn't the right time yet! I know that it's frustrating when we pray and God seems to turn a deaf ear to our cries for help. But people! Things aren't always as they seem. God hears our cries even before we call, and He has the right answer for every situation. He waits on purpose just like He did in so many of the stories in the Bible. That might not make you feel good, but it is what it is. There's always a good reason why God doesn't answer our prayers right away, and it's imperative that we trust Him to do right by us no matter what. God has a set time to answer our prayers, but He waits because it's not the right time—yet!

CHAPTER 3

Say Goodbye to the Past

Philippians 3:13 says, "Brethren, I do not count myself to have apprehended; but one thing I do, forgetting those things which are behind, and reaching forward to those things which are ahead."

Let Go of the Past

Do you know that we can actually find comfort in the past? For some people, hanging on to past hurts and disappointments can become like a security blanket to wrap up your pain and broken dreams in. Sometimes, it's even a lot easier for us to wallow in self-pity because we've become so accustomed to the feelings that we get from it. In a strange sort of way, it serves as an excuse from letting go of the past and moving forward toward the unknown of the future. After the twins were born, I named them Adam George and Andrew Lee Dixon, born August 4, 1988, and died August 5, 1988. Although they lived only twelve hours, they left a gaping hole, the size of China, in my heart for eight years.

This wound was bigger than life and heavier than any burdens I had ever borne. I refused to be comforted because I didn't want anyone, including myself, to minimize their existence. They were real; I carried them, I touched them, I gave them life, and they were just as important to me as my daughter was. Although I wanted another child, a son, Jordan Anthony Lee Dixon, the name that I had chosen years ago for the son I knew God would give me one day, I refused to give that name to one of the twins. I couldn't bear the thought of watching another one of my dreams die. Even in my brokenness, I knew that God wanted to write the ending to this chapter in my life, but I was frightened.

Do It Afraid If You Have To

Before I lost the twins, we were living in a rental property. My husband had a friend that owned a big beautiful house, and he had allowed us to rent it. It was a mother-in-law setup where my mother occupied the lower level, and my husband and I occupied the main level. It was the perfect house for us; we loved it so much that we had planned to purchase it from the owner just as soon as we had enough money for the down payment. About a year prior, my husband was in a really bad car accident, and we were waiting on the insurance company to settle a claim that we had filed. The money from the settlement would have been enough for the down payment to buy our dream house. It was a fairly new house, maybe about three years old, and it was ideal for a young couple just starting out and raising a family. Unfortunately, the owner approached us with an offer to sell while I was in the hospital giving birth to the twins. Everything was happening all at the same time, and we had not yet received the money from the insurance company. My husband had to tell the owner that we couldn't afford to buy the house, so he had no other choice but to list the house for sale.

There we were in the process of making funeral arrangements to bury our children while doing our best to cooperate with the real estate agent that was showing the house—our dream house. My life felt like I was caught up in a whirlwind and nothing at all made any sense. I had just lost one dream, my twins, and I was about to lose another—my dream house. All these losses, all at once; I thought to myself, the only thing left to lose was my mind. There were so many people going in and out of my house that it didn't feel like home anymore. I barely held it together during the funeral. The money from the insurance company finally came in, but it hadn't until after my dream house was sold.

Have you ever wondered what God is doing? I have—all the time. God knew how much we wanted to buy the house that we were living in, but the money came in only weeks after the house was sold. Why didn't God bring in the money before the house was sold so that we didn't have to move? Instead, He allowed me to go through all that chaos of planning a funeral and grieving the loss of my babies while our home was being sold right out from underneath us. I don't understand God at all! The only good thing that came out of it all was the real estate agent that was showing the house. She was a wonderful Christian woman who helped me tremendously during that time. She found out from the owners that I had just lost my babies, and every time she called to make an appointment to show the house, she would always say something encouraging to me. Come to find out later that she too had lost twin girls. We had a common bond—a bond that eventually turned into a friendship.

After the funeral, we had to quickly find another place to live. The house that we were living in had been sold quickly, and we had to vacate within a month. Talk about when it rains, it pours. I was so broken up that I couldn't see straight. I had just suffered the greatest loss of my entire life, and on top of that, we had lost our home and had to move. If it hadn't been for my husband running around, trying to find another place for us to live, I don't know what would have happened to us. Thank God we found something temporary to rent until we were able to purchase a house of our own. We lived there for only six months before we finally found a house that we could afford to buy.

While we were in the process of moving into our house, something strange happened. I was awakened one morning around 3:00 a.m. from a deep sleep. It was almost like someone gently took me by the shoulders and shook me and told me to get up because it was time. At first, I thought that it was my husband that was talking to me, but it wasn't until after I saw him fast asleep beside me that I realized that it was God. I immediately responded by saying, "Time for what?" The voice said, "Time to try again." I knew right away that He was talking to me about trying again to conceive another baby, and to my surprise, I was cooperative. Up to that point, I didn't want to hear anything about having another baby. Although I desperately wanted another son, my Jordan, I was afraid to place myself in another predicament that could potentially blow up in my face.

Joy Comes in the Morning

That morning, something happened to me that I really can't explain. It was as if I was holding my breath for a long time just waiting to exhale. I made love to my husband for the first time since the death of my twins—without fear. Afterward, I knew deep inside my heart that I was going to conceive that morning. Later that evening, when my husband came home from work, I told him what had happened, and he asked me if I thought that I would miraculously become pregnant so soon. I told him that I can't say miraculously; after all, I wasn't the Virgin Mary, but I was absolutely certain that I had already conceived.

Sure enough, I found out that I was pregnant that same month. This pregnancy was the best one out of all the others, in terms of morning sickness. I hardly had any. My decision to use the same ob-gyn that had delivered my daughter and the twins was very unnerving to my entire family, including my husband. They were apprehensive about me using the doctor that was responsible for the death of my twins. At that time, I was filled with anger and resentment toward this man because I believed that it was his mistakes that cost me my dream—my children. It was a holiday weekend and my sister-in-law had invited us to her apartment for the long weekend. Every year on that weekend—Carribana weekend—a multicultural celebration goes on in the city of Toronto.

People from all over the world usually come and party like party animals all weekend. Although I was only twenty-four weeks pregnant, I looked like I was nine months along. I could barely walk due to the extra weight of carrying twins. My daughter was only a year old, and trying to keep up with a toddler in my condition was impossible! I told my husband that I didn't want to go anywhere, except into my favorite pajamas and underneath my favorite comforter with a good book and a cup of herbal tea. But my sister-in-law insisted, and my husband agreed reluctantly. That same night, after we left the celebration and went back to her apartment, I felt strangely tired. I had turned in to bed a little earlier than normal because the twins were more active than normal.

Except for them playing soccer with my bladder all night, I wasn't concerned at all. And as exhausted as I was, I couldn't sleep because I kept going to the bathroom every five minutes. It felt like I had wet the bed, but I hadn't. Soon I realized that something was wrong, and I woke up my husband and asked him to take me home right away. My husband drove like a maniac over ninety kilometers back to the city where we lived and straight to the nearest hospital. There was something wrong with the pregnancy, but my ob-gyn was adamant that everything was fine and reassured me that the babies weren't at risk. He diagnosed my condition as having an infection, but due to my delicate condition, I was admitted to the hospital immediately. I was placed on antibiotics to treat an infection that never existed when in fact, there was a small tear in the embryonic sac and I was losing amniotic fluid. During that week, my condition worsened, and I went into premature labor, and my babies died.

I will never forget the look on the doctor's face when he came into my room after he was notified that I was in labor. He looked at me with such sadness in his eyes and said, "Althea, I am sorry." I ask him if the babies were going to make it, and he said no. I knew in my heart that he was sincere, and I had to find a way to forgive him. My decision to go back to the same doctor six months later was the only way I could forgive him and release him from the liability of causing the death of my children. Even though I was being pressured into filing a lawsuit for negligence, I couldn't, in all good conscience, seek revenge for something that I knew to be a genuine mistake.

He was an excellent ob-gyn and was well respected in the medical community. And furthermore, I liked him. He assumed full responsibility for the deaths of my children, and he didn't try to weasel his way out of it. Most doctors wouldn't have done that, but he did, and I respected his honesty. He was shocked when I walked into his office six months later. It was as if he had seen a ghost! The look on his face was suspect of my true motives of placing myself and another one of my unborn babies into his care again after his mistakes had cost me so much already. He was probably wondering why I hadn't sued him in the first place. It was the wisest decision I had ever made. His prenatal care was exceptional; I couldn't have been in better hands.

Nine and a half months later, on November 24, 1989, I gave birth to a nine-pound, six-ounce baby boy name, Jordan Anthony Lee Dixon. Although this was my fourth child, the birth of this child was unlike anything that I had ever experienced. As a mother who loves all of her children equally and unconditionally, I wouldn't want to minimize the entire firstborn experience at all because for us women, it's a life-changing experience in itself. But on November 24, 1989, when I gave birth to my fourth child, the child that came after the tragic premature deaths of my twins, I felt renewed!

I was hopeful that this baby would help me to get past the pain and agony that was still gnawing in my soul, but unfortunately, that renewed experience lingered briefly like sunlight. Even though I was holding this beautiful baby boy, knowing that God had given me another child, not just another child, a son! Deep down inside of me, I was still in pain, and I didn't know what to do. I was holding my newborn baby in my arms—yet my arms were still aching to hold my twins. I was crying tears of joy mixed with sorrow. Bittersweet emotions flooded my soul. I thought that this baby would erase the pain or, at the very least, eased it a bit, but I was still weeping inside, and I couldn't be comforted. Every time I breast-fed Jordan, I thought about how my milk came in after the birth of the twins but I had no babies to give suck.

And when I held this little boy in my arms and stared into his eyes, I wondered what it would have felt like to hold my two babies in my arms, knowing that I was holding my dream, the childhood dream of a little girl, sitting on the verandah, playing with her dolls, and daydreaming about being the mommy of twins. This baby boy was supposed to be the joy that God had promised me, and although he was, I just couldn't let go of the past. I was still suspended in time. Subconsciously, I had convinced myself that if I were to let go of the twins, this new baby would fill up that void and cause me to forget them, and I didn't want to forget my sons. I needed to keep them alive in my heart and mind forever. This time, I left the hospital with my arms full, but my heart was still heavy. Something was missing. I didn't feel whole!

The first night home from the hospital with my brand-new baby boy felt unreal. I felt like I was wide awake in a dream. I was anxious! I must have held him all night in my arms, watching him breathe; my little miracle baby, I called him. I just couldn't put him down. I was afraid! I thought that if I were to put him down, he would disappear. And when I finally did, he slept beside me in our bed. My husband almost had to sleep in the baby's crib because the crib was always empty. And to be perfectly honest with you, my husband wouldn't have had any problems fitting into that crib quite comfortably—seeing that he's so small and all. I wasn't about to let my baby out of my sight, not even for a second. I wanted to make sure that my baby was safe. And if anything should ever happen, God forbid, I would be right there to stop it. I was not about to lose another child, not if I could help it—so I thought.

As the weeks went by, I was starting to settle down a bit. The initial fear that was sapping my joy when I first came home from the hospital was waning. God was putting his finger on what was wrong in my heart, and I was ready to embrace the truth. The truth was, I was afraid to trust God again, only to have Him disappoint me—again! He had allowed my twins to die, and I just couldn't afford to go down that road again. My doctor may have made a grave mistake when he diagnosed my condition incorrectly, but God doesn't make mistakes. He saw what was going to happen, and He didn't stop it. Now I was broken, and having another child wasn't going to fix me. It wasn't that simple!

I had deep emotional wounds, and I needed help! I must admit though that Jordan was an adorable baby. He was like two babies all rolled up into one. Did I mention that he was nine pounds four ounces at birth? He was this big little ball of sunshine. The nurses at the hospital where he was born called him Muhammad Ali, after the heavyweight fighter. He was such a quiet soul. He never cried unless he was wet or hungry. He never gave me any problems, even to this day. He was pure joy! God told me in my dream that weeping would only be for a night, but joy would come in the morning.

Not Again!

The joy only lasted for seven months after Jordan was born until tragedy struck again. I had just returned to work after being off on maternity leave for over a year when I found out that I was pregnant again. I was not planning on becoming pregnant so quickly. After all, I had just had a baby seven months ago, and my body was worn out from all the stress of the previous pregnancies. I was exhausted! Although being a mother meant everything to me and I found it quite rewarding, I was really looking forward to getting back to work so that I could help my husband with all the bills that were piling up. We had just bought our first house only a few months before Jordan was born, and unfortunately, living on one salary had become a thing of the past. I remember when I was growing up; it was almost a law for women to stay at home and take care of their children.

Very seldom would you find women juggling home and a career, especially growing up in Jamaica. Almost all the women were homemakers to their immediate family and caregivers to their parents, and even grandparents. The news of the pregnancy was not welcomed. But by then, I had come to realize that things don't always happen the way we plan. I was discouraged about the pregnancy that I cried almost every day. In the beginning, I almost drove myself crazy, worrying about how we were going to make ends meet with another baby on the way.

Then one day, I decided to stop crying and face the reality of the situation. I was going to have another baby whether it was planned or not. It wasn't like my husband and I hadn't talked about having another child one day. I guess that one day had just come a lot sooner than we had anticipated. Finally, we came to the conclusion that maybe it was God's will to give us this child a little sooner. I was starting to look forward to having another little boy or girl or maybe even twins again, but I was wrong again!

Only a few months into the pregnancy, I found out that the baby I was carrying was dead. I should have known right away that something was terribly wrong with the pregnancy because it was different. It was nothing like the others. It was too good to be true! I had no morning sickness or bleeding at all. That was rather strange for me because with my other pregnancies, I was sick all the time. But with this pregnancy, I felt as healthy as a horse. I ate everything that I could get my hands on, and I even gained a little weight, which I never did in the first trimester.

I kept on working at my job, which was a first for me. I just thought that this last pregnancy was going to be a lot easier on me. But never in my wildest dream did it ever cross my mind that my baby was dead. After my first ultrasound, my doctor told me that there was no fetal heartbeat and my baby was dead! I didn't believe it. I refused to believe that I had lost another child again! I told myself that God couldn't be that heartless as to put me through all this hell—again. I built a wall around myself in hopes of drowning out all the voices that were telling me that my baby was dead. Even after the doctor had scheduled a D&C, I refused it. I had totally convinced myself that God was not going to let this happen to me again.

My family pleaded with me to have the operation, but I wouldn't listen. After a week of turning a deaf ear to everyone, I started hemorrhaging. Even after I almost bled to death, I still wouldn't listen. Finally, my husband convinced me to do the procedure, and I agreed. I knew from past experience that it was standard procedure for the doctor to do another ultrasound before performing the operation just to be sure that the pregnancy wasn't viable. I was certain that the ultrasound would prove that my baby was alive and it was all a mistake, but it wasn't. The final ultrasound showed that the pregnancy wasn't viable, so I had to have the operation.

I was sobbing when my doctor gave the anesthesiologist the go-ahead to put me to sleep. I started counting backward from ten, but I only got to eight before I was out like light. When I regained consciousness and realized that it was all over, I wanted to die. *Why is this happening to me again?* I thought. *God, I trusted you,* I thought for sure, again, just like it was with the twins that my baby wasn't going to die. After all, my Heavenly Father was in control of my life and He orders my footsteps. Surely, He wouldn't allow me to suffer the same fate again. It was bad enough that my heart hadn't healed from the loss of the twins, and to be dealing with the loss of another child was unkind.

I left the hospital feeling lost and hopeless—again. Those feelings were starting to become all too familiar. I felt like an orphan in a sandstorm. There was no rhyme or reason as to why God was allowing me to suffer in such a merciless way. I just couldn't understand it! This time, I had two children to care for, and I didn't know how. It was my mother again who stepped in and took care of all of us. I have found in my experience that when you're going through a crisis, only one, or if you're lucky, just a handful of people who can truly give you the kind of emotional support that you need.

I had two friends like that, friends with wings; they were my mother and my husband. These friends were always there for me no matter what! My mother and my husband supported me when I lost the twins, and they were there for me again. This was the third time I had lost a child, and it was demoralizing. At least, the first miscarriage, at seventeen years old was my own stupidity and rebellion, but what was the purpose of all this now? I wasn't that naive little girl anymore; I was a responsible married woman, who loved God with all my heart and was doing my best to live a good Christian life. But in spite of that, I was losing my children, one by one, and these losses were irreplaceable! But it didn't matter how many tears I had shed or how much pain I was in; God wasn't doing anything to stop it!

The next couple of months seemed like one continuous nightmare that wouldn't end. You know how when you're having a bad dream and sometimes you can force yourself to wake up right before you fall off a cliff or before someone kill you? That's how I felt for a very long time. I desperately wanted to awaken myself from this nightmare but I couldn't. I felt like I had fallen into a huge crater in the ground and was in this constant state of falling with no end in sight. For a long time, I wasn't able to tell night from day. I was completely disoriented. Even though all that time had passed, it felt like I was stuck in that one horrible day. I remember my sister-in-law was getting married at that time, and my husband and I were in the wedding party. Although I knew that my sister-in-law was counting on us being in her wedding, I just couldn't deal with all the dress fittings, bridal showers, and rehearsals.

I had to dig deep inside myself to find the strength that I knew in my heart I didn't possess in order to follow through with my commitment. Miraculously, I got through the wedding and all the festivities the best that I could and even smiled pretty for the camera, but it was only the strength of God that glued me together long enough to get me through what seemed like one of the longest days of my entire life. Every time I look at myself in the photographs from that wedding, I can still see the mask that I wore that day. Sometimes, life is going to treat us unkindly, and we're going to find ourselves wondering why bad things happen to good people, but I still believe that every disappointment is for a reason. Even though it might take a very long time before we see what God is doing with our disappointments and how He's working behind the scenes rearranging things in our favor, one day, when the time is right, God will reveal His plans, and when He does, it will amaze us.

God's Lifeline

After yet another miscarriage, I went to a very dark place for a very long time. I couldn't deal with the pain and disappointment that was associated with the loss of another child. This was my third miscarriage, and I had lost five children in total—five children, not five puppies or kittens. I knew in my heart that there had to be a reason for all this suffering and loss and that one day, I would understand why. But right there and then, I needed help! I couldn't take any more! It was as if God had heard me and He sent my pastor, the same pastor that helped me when the twins died. My pastor heard what had happened, and he came to see me. He knew that I was grieving and thought that a change of scenery might just be the thing that I needed to pick up my spirit.

He was putting together a team to go into Mexico to do missionary work, and he thought that maybe I might be interested. I was! It was exactly what I needed. I needed time to try and make sense of the senseless loss of my children. The trip was scheduled to take place in a year, and all the other team members were already selected except for me. I was the last to join and the most grateful. The impending trip had given me something to look forward to, like a lifeline, I guess, and I was grateful for the opportunity to do something to help the less fortunate.

I had learned throughout the years that one of the best ways to overcome grief is to help someone else. All the team members had to learn Spanish and that meant taking Spanish lessons. I knew a little bit of Spanish from when I was a child growing up in Jamaica. It was a part of the school's curriculum. Fortunately for me, I loved the language. I had always thought that Spanish was such a beautiful sensual language; little did I know that one day, it would come in handy. Because I was already familiar with the language, it didn't take too long to excel in it. By the time we were ready to go, I was tutoring some of the other team members. I knew enough Spanish to find my way back to the hotel if I were to get lost in Mexico, which, by the way, I did.

My pastor was our Spanish teacher and guide, and he was fluent in Spanish. He had to learn the language the moment he knew that God had called him as an evangelist and missionary to Mexico. Although he had travelled extensively into many other countries, he had a special love for the Mexican people. That was where he felt the most loved and appreciated. The team spent two weeks travelling all over Mexico, ministering to the locals. From holding church meetings to working with the children in the orphanages and on the garbage dumps, we were well received by the people. The Mexican people were friendly, and their hospitality was awesome! I had never seen such humility before. The little that they had, they were eager to share it with us, and their hunger for the gospel was phenomenal.

My Testimony

While I was in Mexico, I was asked to speak to a group of women in one of the evening services. I was asked to share my testimony of how I came to know Jesus as my personal savior. Our pastor had split the group into two, and we ministered in two separate churches that evening. I was a nervous wreck. I had never considered myself to be a speaker by any means, but I have never shied away from talking about God whenever I was asked. I was on the platform a very long time while the people sang hymns in Spanish. Some of them I recognized by the melody because the melody is the same no matter what the language.

The voices of the Spanish people sounded like a great thunder in the heavens. In that moment, I wondered if maybe this is how heaven will be when people from all races get together to praise God. It was magnificent! Before it was my turn to speak, I kept asking God what He wanted me to talk about, but I never heard anything. I thought to myself that when it came time for me to speak, God will answer me then. Soon the worship part of the service was fading, and the pastor took the microphone to introduce me. It was then I sensed inside my heart that God wanted me to talk about the death of the twins. Before I had time to gather my thoughts, the microphone was in my hand, and everyone was staring at me, eagerly waiting for me to say something.

I shared briefly about the life and death of my twins, and as I was speaking, I could see the tears running down the women's faces. I knew that there were many women grieving the loss of someone they loved. I had become familiar with the many faces of grief because it had held me hostage for what seemed like a lifetime. Now God was using the most painful tragedy of my entire life to bring healing and restoration to others. Before the service concluded, the women practically ran to the altar, some standing, some kneeling, while others buried their faces in the pews and bawled. Our team gathered around them and prayed for these wives, mothers, sisters, grandmothers that were weeping for their loved ones. It was so amazing to see the genuine outpouring of affection among these women as they comforted one another.

I mentioned before about working with the children on the dumps. In Mexico, there are families living on the garbage dumps. Literal families—mothers, fathers, and children build their houses out of garbage. To see little children, four or five years old, sifting through the garbage for whatever they can find to eat was gut-wrenching. Missionaries have come in and build houses and schools to educate both the parents and the children right there on the dump. I saw people living under deplorable human conditions that never complained and bellyached like we do in Canada. Whatever you give or do for them is much appreciated no matter how small or large. We could learn a lesson or two on humility of the Spanish people. I said Spanish people because I went to Cuba two times, and the Cubans are pretty much the same when it comes to humility! They may be poor in worldly possessions but certainly not in Spirit. They appeared to be happy and contented in whatever state they're in. I returned home a change woman—so I thought! I was tired of grieving. My life had become a pool of grief, and I was ready to let go of the ashes—but like they say, "Easier said than done."

Let Go of the Ashes

Eight years had come and gone since the birth of my fourth child, Jordan, and I was still consumed with pain and grief over the loss of my twins. By now, my husband was completely fed up with what seemed like a total lack of desire on my part to let go of the past and move on. I never blamed him for feeling fed up with me because I was fed up with me too. As much as I was desperate to let go of the grief and move on with my life,

I think that subconsciously, my refusal to relinquish the pain had become like a pacifier in some way.

Maybe in a strange kind of way, I found it a lot easier or, should I say, a lot safer to live in the past than to face the unknowns of the future. To everyone, I had appeared to be a happily married woman with two beautiful children. I had a wonderful husband that provided well for me, and my children had the best father that any children could ever have. I lived in a nice house with all the material comforts that I needed, yet I felt like something significant was missing from my life. I felt fractured. I didn't feel whole! I cried out to God every day to help me, but nothing happened, or so it seemed. I didn't feel like I was any closer to being healed from these heart wounds than I was years earlier when it first happened.

I Will Not Restore

One day, I just came out and asked God if He was ever going to give me twins again. Something in me needed to know the truth, no matter what. But was I prepared to hear the truth? Sometimes we ask God a question, but when we get an answer, especially one that we're not prepared to hear, we can't accept it. I received one of those answers, one that I wasn't prepared to hear. God told me that He was not going to restore what I had lost but that He wanted to do a new thing. Then on top of that, He told me something else that was unthinkable! God told me to pack up all the things that belonged to the twins and destroy them. When I heard that, it felt like someone had plunged a knife straight into my already wounded heart.

At that moment, I thought I was hearing things, but I wasn't! I know what God's voice sounds like, and it was God. I said to myself, "How in the world could God ask me to do such a thing?" I had already lost so much, and now, He was asking me to give up all that I had left of my babies. All I had were the few little things that the nurses at the hospital gave me after they died. I had the two little bonnets that they wore while they were fighting for their lives in the neonatal unit, two identification bracelets with the names, Baby Boy A and Baby Boy B, and a couple of pictures of them that were taken moments after they died, which I discarded immediately after I saw that they were taken after their death.

I didn't want to look at those pictures to keep reminding me what death looks like. The other items I kept; that was all I had left of them except for the permanent footprints that they left in my heart and soul. Now, it felt like God was telling me to discard them as if they never existed at all. I couldn't do it! The mere thought of it was unheard of! How could any mother throw away every reminder of her children? That was what God was asking me to do.

I fought the impressions of that still, soft, but overwhelming voice of God for a while, but I knew in my heart that I had to be obedient. I knew that it was a waste of time and energy to resist Him because He was not going to go away. The Bible said that if we resist the devil, he will flee. But that doesn't work as far as God is concerned. I found that the more I resisted God, the more He pursued me. After a while, I called my pastor and asked his advice about what I should do. He advised me to do only what I truly felt in my heart to do. With much pain and anguish in my soul, I discarded every reminder that I had of the twins and wept sorely! I wept so hard that day that I thought I was going to be swept away in a pool of my own tears.

Sometimes, we hang on to the very things that God wants us to let go of. And although we know deep inside our heart that we have to let go of the past, we just can't! I know this because of the countless times that I have tried and failed miserably! Not because I didn't desperately wanted to, but only because I just didn't know how. There is no set amount of a time to grieve; it's a personal thing. But to grieve forever would be such a waste, a waste to allow ourselves to get hung up on a loss or disappointment when God has so much more for us. At some point, we have to get up and start living again. We have to let go of the past—past disappointments, past failures, and past losses.

We have to trade in our broken dreams for new ones and move forward into the future that God has for us, knowing that there is absolutely nothing we can do to change our past. We can't move forward when we're looking backward. Quit looking backward, God has more in our future than what we've lost in our past. Look to the horizon; it's a new day. Ask God to help you to let go of the ashes. The Bible tells us that God wants to give us beauty for ashes. In other words, He wants us to relinquish everything that is broken in our lives to Him so that He can give us beauty instead. He is the only one that can turn our mourning into laughter. I did exactly that when I made the decision to destroy everything that I had left of the twins. I took that first step of faith. I figured that if God had truly spoken to me, it would only be a matter of time before my heart would finally heal.

A New Thing

God had spoken, and the answer was no. Just like that, any hope of giving birth to another set of twins was gone. Gone forever! And there was nothing I could have done to change God's mind. It took a long time to finally settle the matter once and for all in my mind and in my heart. But I eventually did. After some time, I mustered up enough courage to asked God for something else. I thought that since He had said no to my request to having another set of twins, surely He wouldn't deny me this.

I wanted another child, and this was going to be my last child—a little girl that looks just like me. And I was going to name her after one of my dearest friends. Since my other two children looks just like my husband, I thought that it would only be fair if this last child looks just like me. After all, I was the one doing all the hard work. In the beginning, my husband and I had lots of fun trying, but after the first three years, I wasn't sure if God was ever going to answer my prayers. Even after my doctor had reassured me that there were no physical reasons why I couldn't conceive; I just hadn't. At that moment, I knew I had to do something, but I didn't know what.

The Fast

One day, I was reading my Bible, and I came across a story about how Jesus would disappear for days and go off by himself to fast and pray. I immediately got the idea that if Jesus had the need to fast and pray to His Father, then I could do the same. After all, I was doing everything that I knew to do to become pregnant, but I wasn't. At this point, the only person that was having the time of his life trying was my husband. As far as he was concerned, it could have gone on indefinitely. This was now almost eight years of trying, *and* I was becoming desperate. I was thirty-seven years old, and time was running out. I made a decision to fast for three days and three nights without food and water. It's considered safe to fast food for a period of time but not water because of the risk of dehydration. But I was desperate! I needed answers, and I was going to get it dead or alive! I chose the week that I was going to fast, and I didn't tell anyone, not even my husband. I took that week off from work and secretly started to fast. I had a husband and two children to care for, and that meant cooking and cleaning, but I didn't care. I wanted another child, and I was determined to get it.

The first day of the fast went a lot better than I had expected. My husband went to work, as usual, and I dropped off my children at school and went straight home. I had planned on spending the next three days doing as little housework as possible. I only answered the telephone if I thought that it was either my husband or my children's school calling. Other than that, I didn't want to be disturbed at all. This was my intimate time alone with God, and that meant spending a lot of time alone praying, reading my Bible, and meditating. Everything was going better than I had expected until I reached day number 2. By then, I was getting weaker and a lot more fatigued physically, but emotionally and spiritually, I felt strong. By the time the third day rolled around, I knew in my heart that something had happened. To this day, my husband still doesn't know anything about the fast, but it worked. Fasting and prayer really does work. I believe that it moves the hand of God to work on our behalf a lot quicker. Within a couple of months after the fast, I became pregnant after eight years of trying.

Only six weeks into the pregnancy and what I had feared the most had come upon me. I was sick again. This time it was worse than all of my other pregnancies combined. It was that bad! I remember one day when my mother came over to help me with my two other children, I was so weak and dehydrated that I could barely stand up. I had lost so much weight that I was just skin and bones with eyes. My husband had just come home from work and found me lying on the floor curled up in my mother's arms—sobbing uncontrollably! As soon as he saw me, he got on the telephone immediately and called my ob-gyn. While he was on the telephone with my doctor making arrangements to have me hospitalized, I told my mother that I wasn't strong enough to go through with the pregnancy. I don't know if I was hallucinating or not, but I remember saying to my mother, "Mama, I can't do this. I can't have this baby."

She thought that I was trying to tell her that I wanted to terminate the pregnancy, but that wasn't what I meant at all. Actually, I had no idea what I meant except that I truly believed that I was going to die with this pregnancy. It was that horrific! My mother held me up while my husband dressed me to go to the hospital. I was in the hospital for weeks before my doctor finally found a medication that worked somewhat. With this medication, I was finally able to keep my food down a lot longer, but I wasn't gaining any weight. I had already lost twenty pounds in the first trimester and looked like I had a severe case of anorexia nervosa, but miraculously, my baby was thriving. God was taking care of both of us. If it hadn't been for God and the love and support of my family, I would have lost my mind.

This Too Shall Pass

One night in particular, I was awake most of the night, vomiting and wetting the bed. Every time I would vomit, I would wet myself from the pressure of the baby sitting on my bladder. The night in question, I was vomiting so much that my bed was completely soaked with vomit and urine. There had been a shortage of nurses working that night, and the ones that were on duty were all tied up in delivery. I must have worn out the call button just trying to get one of the nurses to come and help me, but nobody came. After lying in my own vomit and urine for a while, I realized that no one was coming, and I had to find a way to get out of bed and clean up myself.

The tears were streaming down my face as I stumbled around in the dark, trying to find the bathroom to empty the bedpan that contained my supper from earlier that evening. I made it to the bathroom, cleaned up myself, and proceeded to find clean linen for my bed. The room that I was in was huge! There were three other women in there with me. Even though I tried my best not to disturb the others, I knew that they had to have heard all the commotion I was making. I wasn't certain of it until the next morning when the nurse pulled back the curtains, and one of the ladies said the strangest thing to me. She said, "Dear, this too shall pass."

When I heard those words, I immediately started to cry. This woman was in her third trimester, and she was hospitalized for high blood pressure. Her words of encouragement lifted my spirit and gave me hope that one day the suffering was going to pass. I was the only one in the room that was in my first trimester. All the other women were just about ready to deliver. I couldn't see past the suffering I was in. All I was focused on were the six months of hell that was ahead of me. I was scared stiff!

I couldn't envision me having the baby any time in the near future. But those words of encouragement kept me going one day at a time. I watched every one of the women gave birth one at a time and left me behind in the hospital. I was green with envy as I watched them being wheeled out of the hospital with their babies in their arms and went home. All I wanted was for my turn to come so that I could go home with my baby too, but I had six more months to go, and the thought of another six months felt like an eternity! It was unbearable! I clung to the words of inspiration that the woman gave me. It was all I had, and I needed something. I needed an anchor.

Finally, after several weeks, it was my turn to go home. I felt like a prisoner being released from solitary confinement. It was surreal! I was just entering the second trimester of the pregnancy and most of the morning sickness had passed. I don't know why it's called, "morning sickness" because I was sick morning, noon, and night. I know women that eat whatever they want, get fat, and have a baby. But I, on the other hand, couldn't stop vomiting, lost a lot of weight, and spent most of my pregnancies hospitalized. I don't know why my body has such a difficult time carrying children, but it does! Surprisingly, the next four months went by without any complications at all. My baby boy was developing normally inside of me, and I was feeling optimistic. Yes, my baby boy! The ultrasound confirmed my suspicions, and I wasn't jumping for joy either. I knew all along that it was a boy, and it wasn't my woman's intuition that told me. And my ob-gyn confirmed it after he heard the baby's heart rate. Apparently, girls have a faster heart rate than boys.

Both of us were right! I had a premature baby boy. Seven months into the pregnancy, the unexpected happened. I became very ill and was hospitalized again! This time, I wasn't going home until after the birth of my son in two months. But after a month in the hospital, my doctor had to induce labor and delivered the baby early. My son Philip Jeremy Lee Dixon was born on August 1, 1997, three weeks early. My baby was a little smaller than my other children—but otherwise, he was perfectly healthy. On the other hand, I had developed some complications during delivery and almost died. God intervened again and saved my life. I stayed in the hospital another couple of weeks and was then released. God had now given me three beautiful children, one girl and two boys. I had buried two boys, and now, God had given me two more. My two boys weren't a replacement for my twins by any means. I remember someone telling me that after Philip was born. I knew this person meant well, but it wasn't true. People are irreplaceable! There are some losses that cannot be replaced, and we must accept them and move forward.

It's Not a Girl!

I had asked God for a little girl, but He gave me another baby boy. At first, the baby looked just like me, but within weeks, he started to change drastically. This baby was the splitting image of my husband. God has a sense of humor. He looked more like my husband than all my other children—combined. Because I didn't get the little girl that I wanted, I couldn't use the name that I had picked out. Once again, I didn't get what I wanted, and I didn't know why! I had no other choice but to trust God and move on, like I had done with the twins. A couple of years later, my friend, the one that I was going to name my baby after, ended the friendship. After the friendship ended, I was relieved that the baby was a boy and that I hadn't used the name because if I had, the name would have been a constant reminder of the hurt. The Bible said that God's ways are higher than our ways, and His thoughts are higher than our thoughts. Let's face it, we're not going to get everything we want in life, but every disappointment is for a reason—whether we understand it or even agree with it. God knows the future, and He sees what's around the corner. He knows how everything is going to turn out, and He already has the solution to every one of our problems.

CHAPTER 4

Dreams and Visions

> And it shall come to pass afterward, That I will pour out My Spirit on all flesh; Your sons and your daughters shall prophesy, Your old men shall dream dreams, Your young men shall see visions.
>
> —Joel 2:28 (NKJ)

What Is a Dream?

The word *dream* has multiple meanings, but I am only going to talk about two: "a series of thoughts, images, or emotions occurring during sleep" and "a strongly desired goal or purpose." First, let's take a look at the ones that occurs while we sleep. There are two kinds of dreams that are products of sleep: 1.) spiritual dreams—the ones that come from God. These dreams are one of the many spiritual gifts from God to us. For God uses them to reveal His will and plans for our lives and 2.) natural dreams—the ones that our mind produces. Although it has been said that all natural dreams are just figments of our imaginations, some are known to actually come from God and should not be easily discarded. Paul McCartney, one of the members of the Beatles, had a dream. I believe that his dream was a spiritual dream given to him by God, and I believe this because it came to pass.

According to biographers of McCartney and the Beatles, McCartney composed the entire melody in a dream one night in his room at the Wimpole Street home of his then girlfriend Jane Asher and her family. Upon waking, he hurried to a piano and played the tune to avoid forgetting it. McCartney's initial concern was that he had subconsciously plagiarized someone else's work (known as cryptomnesia). As he put it, "For about a month, I went round to people in the music business and asked them whether they had ever heard it before. Eventually it became like handing something in to the police. I thought if no one claimed it after a few weeks, then I could have it." Upon being convinced that he had not robbed anyone of his melody, McCartney began writing lyrics to suit it.

Another famous spiritual dream was that of President Abraham Lincoln shortly before his assassination. The extraordinary details of Abraham Lincoln's prophetic dream are recorded in "Recollections of Abraham Lincoln, 1847-1885" (Ward Hill Lamon, 1911):

About ten days ago, I retired very late. I had been up waiting for important dispatches from the front. I could not have been long in bed when I fell into a slumber, for I was weary. I soon began to dream. There seemed to be a death-like stillness about me. Then I heard subdued sobs, as if a number of people were weeping. I thought I left my bed and wandered downstairs. There the silence was broken by the same pitiful sobbing, but the mourners were invisible. I went from room to room; no living person was in sight, but the same mournful sounds of distress met me as I passed along. It was light in all the rooms; every object was familiar to me; but where were all the people who were grieving as if their hearts would break?

I was puzzled and alarmed. What could be the meaning of all this? Determined to find the cause of a state of things so mysterious and so shocking, I kept on until I arrived at the East Room, which I entered. There I met with a sickening surprise. Before me was a catafalque, on which rested a corpse wrapped in funeral vestments. Around it were stationed soldiers who were acting as guards; and there was a throng of people, some gazing mournfully upon the corpse, whose face was covered, others weeping pitifully. "Who is dead in the White House?" I demanded of one of the soldiers. "The President" was his answer; "he was killed by an assassin!" Then came a loud burst of grief from the crowd, which awoke me from my dream.

After President Lincoln's assassination, his casket was, in fact, put on a platform in the East Room where soldiers were stationed to act as guards. Dreams are far from meaningless fantasy or random neurological discharge. They are direct communications from the source of being which guide us, grow us, enrich us, and on sad occasion, forewarn us of events destined to change the world.

I totally agree with the author. This confirms that dreams and visions are very important. They allow us to access information from the past, present, and future—all at the same time. Unfortunately, dreams can either bless or torment us. Bless us if we understand the messages and heed them, or torment us when we don't know how to interpret them and ignore them.

I Have a Dream

"I have a dream." These four little words made famous by the legendary Dr. Martin Luther King Jr. was not a night vision—those dreams that occur while we sleep—but it was a strong goal or hope, that great desire of our life. As in my son Jordan, dream of playing professional basketball. Every person on this planet dreams, whether in their sleep, like Paul McCartney and President Abraham Lincoln or in their soul like Dr. Martin Luther King Jr. or both. I also had a dream. I had a dream, like Dr. Martin Luther King Jr. As in I had a great desire in my soul to have twins. And I had a spiritual dream, like Paul McCartney and President Abraham Lincoln. But only one of my dreams came true. I am a dreamer of dreams and have been dreaming spiritual dreams ever since I was a child. I was considered to be a gifted child. I would see the past, present, and future in my dreams, and most of the time, they would come to pass almost identical to the way I had seen them.

I was always fascinated with my own dreams and those of others, but I didn't always know how to interpret them until I became an adult. At first, I took them literally. But after many years, God taught me how to read symbols and how to recognize the ones that are authentic. Dreams can be very confusing, but God has chosen to use them as a way to communicate with us. Dreams are used to give us insight into the future or to warn us of impending dangers or to bring corrections when we have sinned against God. Whether it's Joseph and Pharaoh in the Bible or to countless others, like President Abraham Lincoln, Paul McCartney, and me, God is the one who chooses to communicate to us as He sees fit.

I believe that President Abraham Lincoln's dream was no ordinary dream. It was a spiritual dream given to him by God to warn him about his own death. Maybe had he paid attention to the warning, he might not have been assassinated. God saw what was about to befall the president and tried to warn him, just like He tried to warn me about of the death of my twins. Paying attention to your dreams is imperative! It could be a matter of life or death! I had always wondered why God said no to my dream of having twins, so I thought that it was time to ask Him. One day, I was in my kitchen, standing at the sink, washing the dishes when I ask God why He allowed my twins to die. I was astounded when I heard His reply. God told me that He didn't say no. I replied, "What do you mean you didn't say no? They're dead!" What I heard next shocked me. God told me that He tried to warn me of their premature death, but I didn't heed the warning. When I was five months pregnant with them, I had a dream where Jesus appeared to me and said, "Weeping may endure for the night, but joy comes in the morning." God said that if I had heeded the warning by praying against the tragedy that was about to befall me, it would have averted death, and they would be alive today.

God tried to warn me, but I was ignorant, and my ignorance cost me my dream. How many times have we been warned against impending danger only to miss the warning signs and wind up derailed? I had missed the warning signs, and my babies died. It got me thinking about how many more warning signs I had missed throughout the course of my life? How many more babies or houses or opportunities had I lost because I missed the warning signs? I had always thought that the twins were not a part of God's will for my life, or else, they wouldn't have died. Now God was saying otherwise.

I remember that dream almost like it was yesterday. I was twenty-four weeks pregnant with the twin boys, and like I routinely did every afternoon, I took a nap before lunch. My mother was living downstairs on the lower level of the split-level house we were renting. My mother did everything for me, including meal preparations. I had just woke up and was about to sit down to a bowl of Mama's vegetable soup—that was my favorite craving. I had soup for lunch almost daily. That afternoon, I had a dream that Jesus appeared to me and said, "Weeping may endure for a night, but joy comes in the morning." My mom and I talked all afternoon about what we thought the dream meant but never in our wildest dreams did either one of us thought that it was a warning of any kind to even bother praying about it. We simply dismissed it. That's what God meant when He told me that I didn't heed His warnings. "Weeping" denotes pain and sorrow; the pain and sorrow that would follow the death of my children. To think that if I had known, my children would be alive today.

Sweet Dreams

A dream given by God is a powerful thing. It can ultimately change your personal life and the lives of many others—like President Abraham Lincoln and Paul McCartney. What would have happened if President Lincoln had heeded the warnings in his dream and had not been assassinated? How much that would have changed the course of the United States of America? What about Paul McCartney? What would have happened if he had never written the song "Yesterday"? That song became one of the greatest love songs of all times. It's one of my favorites. And I'm sure that the Beatles made a fortune on that song. When we go to sleep at nights, our body first enters what is called the slumber zone. This is when we're just falling asleep. This zone is usually when God gives us a dream because we're not fast asleep. In this zone, we will most likely remember our dreams in details.

The next zone is called the deep sleep zone. When we enter this zone, we most likely won't remember our dreams at all. We might remember bits and pieces but not enough to make sense of it all. The last zone is called the rest zone. This is when we are completely rested and coming out of the deep sleep zone. If we get a dream in this zone, we will most likely remember it in details, just like we would in the slumber zone. Whenever we get a dream that we think means something, it's better to take it seriously than to just dismiss it as a natural dream. We may not understand it at first, but if we ask God to reveal its mysteries, He will. God desires to give us wisdom and understanding into spiritual matters, but we have to want it and ask for it.

What Is a Vision?

The word *vision* means "something seen in a dream, trance, or ecstasy; a supernatural appearance that conveys a revelation." There are also two kinds of visions: the ones that you get when you are asleep (a night vision) and the ones that you get when you're awake (open visions), like a trance. Both dreams and visions are gifts from God. They are to instruct, reveal, or to prepare us for something. For example, when God gives us a dream or vision about death, it's either to stop it or to prepare us for it. In some cases, even if we heed the warnings by praying against it, it won't stop it! When it is God's will to do something, He's going to do it, and nothing can stop it—not even our prayers. Several years ago, my friend's husband died of cancer. To this day, I really can't say if I had a vision about his death or not.

It was a Sunday morning; I was in the gym, exercising, which I normally don't do on a Sunday. As a devout Christian, every Sunday mornings and evenings are dedicated to church and family. But this particular Sunday, I didn't want to be in church. I had an intense desire to be alone, so I ended up at the gym. I wasn't there more than an hour when all of a sudden, something just came over me, as if I was in a trance. I guess this is what an out-of-body experience feels like. While I was in this trancelike state, I heard a voice speaking to me, but it wasn't audible. It was coming from some place deep inside of me. The voice told me that my friend's husband was going to die—that she was going to be a young widow. I stood there—frozen, like a block of ice! I couldn't move. I couldn't breathe. After I came out of this anomalous fog, I picked up the telephone in the gym and called my friend immediately and told her. Now, that's not something you would normally tell a friend, especially over the phone. You don't just call up one of your friends and say, "Oh, by the way, friend, God told me that your husband is going to die." Up to that point, I had never done anything that outrageous before. But that day, I did! Something strange just came over me.

I had always considered myself to be a kind, sensitive person—that would never hurt someone intentionally. But I had this overwhelming desire to tell her what had happened to me and what I had heard. But what was even more bizarre than telling her that her husband was going to pass away was that she already knew. There I was worrying about how she was going to react to my totally insane prophecy—if that's what it was—when all along, she already knew. Apparently, she had a similar revelation years ago, but she never told anyone until that day. All I did was to confirm what she already knew. Within months, her husband was diagnosed with cancer. Someone that was perfectly healthy, never been sick a day in his life, just started feeling sick, went to the doctor, and was told that he had cancer.

He died two years later. Even though he underwent surgery, radiation therapy, and chemotherapy, he died anyway. Was it a coincidence that we both saw his death years in advance? Even though my friend and I had both heeded the warnings and prayed against it, it didn't avert his death. Even if we had cried a river and begged God to spare his life—and we did—it didn't stop it from happening. Clearly, the warnings were to prepare my friend for the death of her husband, not to forestall it. This is just my opinion. I believe that it was his time to die. I believe that everyone one of us on this planet has an appointment with death. The Bible says in Hebrews 9:27, "And as it is appointed for men to die once, but after this the judgment." It is a fact that some of us will live to a ripe old age and, hopefully, die peaceably in our sleep while others will die young and suffer greatly. Only God knows how and when we are going to die.

I heard an interesting story about a little boy that was in the hospital, dying of a heart disease. In the final days leading up to his death, he asked the doctor a question about God and heaven. The little boy said, "Why is God taking me to heaven?" The doctor was dumbfounded. He hesitated a while, trying his best to compose himself, while fighting back the tears that were welling up in his eyes; he replied, "Son, God is not taking you to heaven, He's receiving you." That's a question that most, if not all of us will never truly know the answer to. Death is a mystery—a very confusing and painful one. We do our best to try and figure out what was in God's mind at the time when He created the human body with the potential to die. Whatever would possess Him to allow such a thing to befall us? Theologians would argue that God didn't create us to die in the first place—that it was man's disobedience that allowed sin to enter the world. And the penalty for sin is death.

Is Suicide Unforgiveable?

I don't get a lot of open visions, maybe only a handful in my entire life, but when I do, they always mean something. I had another strange vision in 1994, only days before my uncle committed suicide. This time, it was a Sunday afternoon—not morning—and I did go to church that morning. Actually, my husband and I gave my mother a ride home from church, like we normally did. When we drove up outside my mother's house, I saw my uncle, which was my mother's older brother, sitting on the front porch. My uncle was visiting my mother from Jamaica, where he had been living for a couple of years after his retirement. He and his wife were living in Canada for many years, but after they retired, they migrated back to Jamaica, where they had planned on spending their golden years soaking up the sunshine and drinking coconut water all day long. It was my uncle who sponsored my mother in 1968, to come to Canada. But unfortunately, he became ill and came back to Canada to see a specialist. As soon as I saw him sitting on the front porch, I saw a vision of his death.

I told my husband on our way home what I had seen. And as soon as I got home, I called my mother and told her. I don't remember what she said or even if she believed me or not, but a couple of weeks later, my uncle went out to a wooded area behind an automotive plant and hung himself. Although I had seen the vision and told my mother that her brother was going to die, I didn't heed the warning. I ignored it! I remembered telling my husband that maybe I was just seeing things. But if I had just heeded the warning by praying for the safety and well-being of my uncle, maybe he wouldn't have died. Unlike the death of my friend's husband, I believe with all of my heart that suicide is not a part of God's will for our lives. There's a huge difference between someone dying from a disease or a tragedy of some kind than to take his/her own life.

Suicide is wrong, and God doesn't condone it, but I believe that He forgives it. Some people can be in so much pain that they actually convince themselves that suicide is their only option. My uncle was such a person. He was sick and in a lot of pain, and maybe, he thought that ending his life would end his pain. Our family was distraught by his suicide. Most religions teach that if someone commits suicide, they don't go to heaven. Their soul is damned to hell. I don't believe that. I believe that God has the final say—not man! I believe that one day, when I go to heaven, I am going to see my uncle there. I don't judge people that commit suicide because I planned my own death by suicide several years ago. And had it not been for God's supernatural intervention, I would have died. I was in so much pain that I planned to end my life in hopes of ending the pain.

It didn't matter that I had a husband and three children, which included a two-year-old baby. I felt hopeless. I just didn't get up one day and plan my own death. It takes time. You plan and rehearse the plan over and over in your mind for a long time—even years. While the pain in your heart gets bigger and bigger until your heart and mind explodes. I couldn't talk to anyone, not even the ones closest to me about what I was thinking. I started isolating myself, spiraling into despondency with each passing day. I tried to find a way out of the pain with self-help books, prayer—even alcohol. And when everything else failed, one day, I dropped off my baby at my mother's house with the intention of going to the cemetery where my twins are buried, take a bottle full of sleeping pills, and go to sleep—permanently.

When I showed up at my mother's house with the baby, right away, she knew something was wrong, but she didn't know what. I got into my car and pointed it into the direction of the cemetery. But what was about to happen saved my life that day. I remember driving toward the cemetery, and all of a sudden, I found myself inside the parking lot at the church. To this day, I don't know how I got there. It was as if someone just picked up my car and dropped it into the parking lot. The last thing I remembered was leaving my mother's house and stopping at a red traffic light. But after that, I have no memory of how I got to the church.

When I realized where I was and that I was still alive, I sat in my car and wept! I knew something miraculous had happened to me that day. I knew that God had stepped in and changed my plans and spared my life.

I went back to my mother's house, picked up my baby, and went home. By then, I was weary and confused. Fear and depression lay thick upon my soul. I put the baby in his crib, went into my bedroom, and lay down on my bed. Curling into a fetal position, I cried so hard that I soon lapsed into an exhausted sleep. While I was sleeping, I had the most incredible dream—a spiritual dream. In my dream, Jesus appeared to me, and He said something, but I can't remember exactly what He said. The only thing I remember is that after I woke up, I was free! All the pain and despair I was in was gone. Jesus walked into my dream and healed my broken heart.

Whatever happened in my dream was a divine visitation from God. This was not the first time Jesus had appeared to me in a dream. Actually, I've had several supernatural encounters with God over the years. That day, I believe God saved my life twice. First, when He intercepted my suicide attempt and, second, when He healed me in my sleep. Why did Jesus save my life but not my uncle's life? Why did He allow my uncle to take his own life when He could have intercepted it? I don't know. Since that day, I have never thought about taking my life again. God healed me from the spirit of suicide.

A Matter of Life or Death

In 2007, I had a dream about my death. I dreamt that I went into a public washroom, and there was a casket behind the door. At first, I didn't see it. I caught a glimpse of it out of my peripheral vision. When I realized what I had seen, I started to run. Suddenly, I heard a woman's voice speaking to me from behind one of the stalls. She said, "Fear not." It stopped me dead in my tracks. She gave me a message to give to my sister who had just lost her husband of twenty-three years to cancer. Then she told me that I was going to die. The next morning, I woke up in a cold sweat. I was terrified! I called my mother and told her about the dream. We prayed against it over and over again for about a week until both of us felt a peace in our hearts that everything was going to be all right. In 2009, out of the blue, I started thinking about the dream all over again. Again, I felt this overpowering fear that I needed to pray some more. I called my mother again, and we prayed against it.

A couple of months later, on October 11, 2009, I suffered a brain aneurysm and almost died! Had I not heeded the warning I had received in a dream, I am convinced that I would have died. I cannot begin to express how crucial dreams and visions are. They actually could be a matter of life or death. I have made important decisions based on dreams because, over the years, I have seen God use my dreams to change my directions when I was headed for trouble or to warn me about something that I normally wouldn't pay much attention to otherwise.

In 2007, I had another dream that I believe to be a spiritual dream. I saw the writing of this book long before its conception. At first, it was just a dream—nothing more. But when my mother told me to keep a journal of my sufferings, I realized that my dream was a spiritual dream and not a natural dream. I dreamt that I was arrested outside my brother's house and handcuffed inside my vehicle by two policemen. The police claimed that I had threatened to kill someone and they had a warrant for my arrest. I kept insisting that I was innocent and that they had the wrong person, but they wouldn't listen. Instead, they left me alone, chained inside my vehicle, and went off somewhere. While I was waiting for them to return, my handcuffs miraculously turned into plastic, and I snapped them asunder and broke free.

Immediately, I exited the vehicle and went inside my brother's house. Upon entering the house, I saw two women visiting with my brother and his wife. When they saw me, they took me back outside to my vehicle and chained me back up again. Before they deserted me, I noticed that one of them had a passport in her hand. I recognized it to be an old expired Jamaican passport of mine. It was the same one that I had when I was arrested at the airport in 1979. I took the passport from her and started going through the pages. I saw photographs of every bad thing that had ever happened to me, including the arrest in 1979. Frozen by what I was looking at, the van door slid open, and it was the police. One of them unshackled me and told me that they had made a mistake, and I was free to go.

I believe the old expired Jamaican passport represents this book. And all the photographs of my life inside of it represent my biography. The handcuffs on my wrists that miraculously turned into plastic represent all the struggles in my past that God delivered me from. Dreams and visions are crucial to our every day lives. God uses them to offer insight and direction into our future. And although all of us dream dreams, unfortunately, not all of us know how to interpret them

Repetitive Dreams

Dreams are like a trailer of a movie. They allow us to see a sneak preview into the future, and they can even show us events from our past that our subconscious minds have blocked out. When we keep getting repetitive dreams, we have to sit up and take notice because they are very important. They are like red flags! They are dreams that we get all the time. Sometimes, it can be the same dream or something similar. Repetitive dreams mean something. In my experience, whenever I keep getting the same dream over and over again, I find that God is trying to get my attention.

The Bible says in Job 33:14-17, "For God may speak in one way or another, yet man does not perceive it. In a dream, in a vision of the night, when deep sleep falls upon men, while slumbering on their beds, then he opens the ears of men, and seals their instructions. In order to turn man from his deed." You can't get it any plainer. When God speak once and we don't get it, He'll speak again and again and again until we get it. That's what repetitive dreams are, God speaking to us as often as it takes until we listen. If you're getting a repetitive dream, especially if it's a disturbing one, ask God to give you the interpretation. You may not get it overnight, but if you commit your dreams to Him, He will reveal the truth to you in time.

I remember one time; I used to get this same dream over and over again. I had been dreaming that same dream at least once or twice a week for years. It had gotten to the point where I was starting to get fed up with these dreams especially because they were quite unsettling and I didn't know what to make of them. One night, I asked God to give me the interpretation. The dreams were about a very dear friend that was always doing something vindictive to hurt me. In my dreams, she would do all these mean things to me, and when I confronted her, she wouldn't apologize. She would justify her bad behavior, which ultimately lead to a parting of our ways. In reality, she is one of my closest friends, so you can just imagine how confused I was.

Not long after I prayed and asked God to reveal the answer to me, He did. Had I known that He would have answered me so quickly, I wouldn't have waited so long to ask. God showed me that her heart wasn't right toward me even though she appeared to be my friend in reality. She was jealous of me, and the dreams were warning me not to trust her. To be perfectly honest with you, I had always had a strange feeling in my gut about her, but I kept ignoring it. I thought that I was being paranoid! Even though I could clearly see that she wasn't supportive of me in my endeavors, I kept trying to make excuses for her because I thought that she was my friend. Whether she's truly my friend but has some jealousy issues or not, it's important enough for God to warn me about her; we still talk, but I'm a lot more careful around her. I'm more careful as to what I say to her, and I don't ask her for any serious advice anymore. This is another story about a repetitive dream that I had about two of my dearest friends.

Foster Parents

A couple of years ago, I had a dream about one of my dearest friends named Dawn. Dawn and her husband Steve are two of the most honest, trust-worthy, beautiful people I have ever met. They have two children—a boy and a girl. But they wanted more. They love children! They wanted a house full of them, but unfortunately, after the birth of their second child, they didn't have any more. Now both of them are in their forties, and it seems unlikely that they're ever going to have any more biological children, but nothing is impossible with God.

After a while, they thought about adoption and started the journey by applying to become foster parents first. Before they told me about their intentions, I had a dream that I saw them with two children that weren't their own. I told Dawn about the dream right away and encouraged her that God was going to bring two more children into their home. After some time had passed and she wasn't getting pregnant and there were no foster children, she was discouraged! That's what waiting will do. Nobody likes to wait.

Sometime later, I had a second dream. I saw Dawn and her husband Steve standing on the platform at their church, dedicating their children. I didn't see the children that were being dedicated, but I knew that it wasn't their two biological children because those children were already dedicated years ago. I was present for both dedications. When I told Dawn about the second dream, we knew that it was a confirmation of the first dream. Finally, about a year later, they became foster parents to two beautiful little girls—two sisters. Repetitive dreams are usually confirmations of the first dream. Don't dismiss them as being worthless—they're not. They're valuable! Heed them or else you may regret it.

See the Invisible, Achieve the Impossible!

Earlier, I talked a bit about the kind of dream that Dr. Martin Luther King Jr. had the one that is a strong goal or desire. This kind of a dreamer has a fixed desire that is the engine of their lives. It's a secret longing of the heart. It's a dream or dreams that burns like hot coals inside your soul. It's the last thing you think about at nights, and the first thing you think about in the mornings. Not all dreams will come true, but I admire the ones who break the womb as a dreamer and will go down into the grave a dreamer. Hats off to those who dare to dream and dream big! We may never achieve all our dreams, but if we don't have any dreams at all, then we will achieve nothing!

My son Jordan is a dreamer, just like his mother, and I love that characteristic about him. From he was knee-high to a grasshopper, Jordan dreamed of playing in the NBA. He played basketball in both elementary and high school and now in college. He has boxes filled with trophies, ribbons, and plaques, honoring his accomplishments over the years. From Rookie of the Year to the Most Valuable Player (MVP) awards, name it—he's got it! When he was in high school, his photographs were always featured in the sports section of the local newspaper. His freshman year in college, he won the Rookie of the Year award and was always being interviewed by the local television station. But even with these awards, he only received one partial scholarship offer to a D3 college in the United States, which he never accepted.

Even though my son's dream seems to be going up in smoke, he still hasn't given up or retreated in anyway, except for one time, which I will talk about a little later. He eats, sleeps, and breathes basketball. It's all he talks about. I understand him so well. He's a chip off my old block. He's the best part of me in every way. My son has laid hold of his dream since he was a boy, and his dream has laid hold on his soul. A true dreamer of dreams never surrenders to anyone or anything but to the giver of the dream—God! I'm not sure if my son believes that his dream to play professional basketball was given to him by God. We've never talked about it. Not all dreams are given to us by God. Sometimes they are our own desires. If you have a dream and you're not sure if your dream is from God, just ask Him. If your dream falls along the wayside, let it go, just like I had to when my twins died. If not, hold it in your heart and let God bring it to pass.

My son Jordan the basketball player, only has one more year left in college. He's the captain of the basketball team and one of, if not, the best player on the team. Every team that he has ever played on, everyone loved him—both the coaches and players. He's kind, dedicated, and respectable. He's one of the most humble people I know, and I'm not saying that because he's my son. But regardless of his numerous accomplishments in basketball, he still hasn't been looked at for anything lucrative. I know the older he gets, the more impossible his chances are of playing professional basketball. Normally, the players get drafted while they are still in high school. Some get drafted in college. My son is in college. You don't usually get picked up by a professional team when you are already twenty-one years old—that's considered to be too old. But I can't bring myself to discourage him to give up his dream. I have to continue to pray and support him in whatever way I can to keep dreaming until God speaks. An anonymous author said, "Hope sees the invisible, feels the intangible, and achieves the impossible." Nothing is impossible with God!

Don't Say a Word

Years ago, I had a dream—a lifelong dream that no one knew about except my husband. I made the worst mistake of my life by telling my dream to a very close friend of mine—not knowing that she wasn't really a friend. Every time we talked on the telephone or went out for coffee, she would ask me a lot of questions about my dream and what I was planning on doing about them, but I didn't have a clue that her intentions were distrustful. By the time I realized that I had foolishly divulged my secrets, it was too late.

She was cunningly extracting information from me without my knowledge and had been using it to steal my dream and to get a jump-start on my plans. But what she didn't know was that God had changed my direction. I didn't tell her about the change in my plans for some time and I didn't know why. I just felt an impression in my heart not to tell anyone, including her. When I finally told her what I was doing and that my plans had changed, she was already in too deep—up to her eyeballs in trouble. My new plans were successful and hers weren't. She was left holding the bag—so to speak. Her deceptions over the years changed our relationship, and in the end, the friendship ended.

When God gives us a dream, I know firsthand how exciting it can be, and keeping it to ourselves can be almost impossible. It's only natural that we would want to share it with someone, especially our family and friends. That's what I did, only to have one of my best friends try to steal my dream. It didn't surprise me to learn that her plans didn't work out because it wasn't her dream—it was mine! You can't take someone else's dream and make it your own. We need to have our own dreams. Not that our dream is so original that nobody else in the world shares the same dream. I'm sure that my son is not the only person in the world that has ever dreamed of playing professional basketball. Just look at all the dreamers that make up the teams in the NBA. But in this case, I know for certain she took my dream and my idea and tried to implement it because she kept it hidden from me for a long time.

When God gives us a dream or maybe it's just our own desires, we need to guard our dreams until they are fulfilled. We have to be extra careful that we just don't blab it to every Tom, Dick, or Harry. Remember what happened to Joseph when he told his own brothers about his dreams? Because they were jealous of him, they tried to destroy his dreams by selling him into slavery. Who would do such an evil thing to their own brother? Then again, the first murder that is recorded in the Bible was between two brothers, Cain and Abel, and jealousy was at the very heart of it. Sad to say, even thousands of years later, jealousy is still destroying relationships because man hasn't evolved since the Garden of Eden.

Wait Patiently on God

Psalms 37:7 says, "Rest in the Lord, and wait patiently for Him." Many years ago, when my husband and I were dating, we used to visit a Christian drop-in center almost every Saturday evening. The center provided a clean, Christian, dating alternative for young people, and we loved going there. Over time, we became friends with the young pastor and his girlfriend, who is now his wife that ran the center. He was a good man that really had a heart to help people—especially homeless people and drug addicts. One time, he told me a story that stirred me tremendously. It was about a passionate dream that he felt God gave to him to help young people. The young pastor was very handy. He had a special gift for making things out of wood, but his specialty was a large grandfather rocking chair that everybody loved. One day, he felt that God gave him the green light to start his own business making these huge grandfather rocking chairs and to hire some of the young people that he had been helping to help him run the business.

The young pastor poured all his personal money into renting a warehouse, buying materials, and hiring a staff. Although his intentions were admirable, in the end, the business failed and he lost everything. I think that letting go his employees was a lot harder on him than all the money he had lost. Was the dream from God? Perhaps! Not because it failed doesn't mean that it wasn't from God. The young pastor learned a very valuable lesson the hard way, one that he most likely will never forget. God gave him a dream, but instead of waiting on God to bring it to pass, he tried to give birth to it and failed miserably! How many times have we been guilty of the same thing?

By the way, this young pastor spent most of his life helping young people, first, as a youth pastor and then as an associate pastor in a small local church. He preached in many churches for over twenty years before he went on to pastor his own church. He is now an evangelist who travels all over the world preaching the gospel and doing missionary work in countries like Cuba, Haiti, Mexico, and others. When God gives us a dream, it's not our responsibility to make it happen—it's God's. Wait on Him! To rush ahead of God, like the young pastor, would be a grave mistake, one that we may regret for a very long time. God never gives us a dream today and bring it to pass tomorrow. It takes time!

God is a God of timing, and His timing is always perfect. He knows when we are ready to step into our destiny. He knows when we are mature enough to handle the responsibilities that goes with the fulfillment of our dreams. Though the process can be agonizing! It's worth the wait. And sometimes, it could take years—like Joseph. Joseph was seventeen years old when God gave him two dreams about his future. But his dreams didn't come to pass until he was thirty years old. It took thirteen years from the time of inception to fulfillment. Thirteen long years! God didn't purposely harness him to frustrate him but to prepare him. In my opinion, the greater the dream, the longer you have to wait.

Take the Limits Off of God

While we are waiting on God, He uses the time to work out the flaws in our character and remove the obstacles that are hindering us from possessing our dreams. This reminds me of another story that I heard about a friend of mine whose husband committed suicide and left her with two small children—two girls. Years later, she met and married a wonderful Christian man and had another child—another girl. She told me how much she desperately wanted a son, but between the two of them, they had three girls, and three children were enough. One day, she told me that God had given her a promise of a son, but she didn't know what to believe considering her age and whether or not it was her own obsession with having a son or not. She reluctantly told her husband what she thought God had said to her, but she was afraid to try again—only to end up with another girl. After careful consideration, they decided not to have another child.

One night, she had a dream, and in her dream, God told her that it was Him that had spoken to her about giving her a son, but the decision to trust Him was solely up to her. God will never strong-arm anyone into doing anything that she/he doesn't want to do. He wants us to obey Him freely because we love Him. She told me how painful it was and how much they struggled with the decision that they had to make, but eventually, she changed her mind and started trying again to become pregnant. Sure enough! It didn't take too long before she turned up pregnant again. Nine months later, she had a beautiful baby boy name Matthew. The name Matthew means "gift from God." What would have happened if my friend and her husband hadn't decided to go back and try again? They would have missed out on the most awesome blessing that God had for them—a son!

This also reminds me of another story, but this one didn't have such a happy ending. This story is about another friend who had always wanted a son—someone to carry on his name. He married a woman with two children—one boy and one girl—but he had no children of his own. Eventually, they had three children together—all girls—but still no boys to carry on his name. I often wondered why having boys are so important to men. Girls can still carry on their father's name you know. I used my maiden name in all three of my children's names. And I still sign my maiden name on official documents. I may have taken my husband's name, but I am going to be a Lee till the day I die. It's in my bloodline—not the name. Over the years, several people, including this man and his wife, all had dreams about them having a beautiful baby boy. But what was so strange about these dreams were everyone dreamed the same baby boy. Their descriptions of the baby boy were all the same right down to the tiniest details. Even I had several dreams about this baby.

The last dream that I had about this baby, I tried emphatically to convince them to go back one last time. I knew in my heart that all the dreams we were getting were not a coincidence. They were spiritual dreams from God. I believed God wanted to give them a son, but they were adamant about not wanting to try again. They had given up. They were both in their forties, and between the both of them, they already had five children. Unfortunately, they never went back, and my friend's dream of having a son never came to pass. Sometimes when we lose our dreams, it's not always because God said no. Sometimes, it's because we say no. And when that happens, we have to live with the consequences of our decisions, and that's not always an easy thing to do.

Success Is Failure Turned Inside Out

How badly do you want your dreams to come true? Do you want it badly enough to fight for it? I have a very dear friend, Beverly, and she reminds me so much of President Abraham Lincoln—she is a fighter! When I read the story of how many times Abraham Lincoln ran for office before he was finally elected in 1860 as the sixteenth president of the United States of America, I was moved to tears. His story made me realize that even a failure can become the president of the most power country in the world. It has been said that success is failure turned inside out. I believe that wholeheartedly! I believe that if you dig your heels in and don't give up on your dreams, you can achieve almost anything. Abraham Lincoln ran for office seven times before he was finally elected. While he was suffering one defeat after another in his professional life, he had many other tragedies in his personal life, including the death of his fiancée. His story has been used by motivational speakers all over the world as a tool to inspire people to overcome life's difficulties.

Never Give Up!

My friend, Beverly—the one that reminds me of Abraham Lincoln—is a remarkable woman. When we first met, she was married and had three children—all girls. She desperately wanted a son. She was obsessed with it. Shortly after we became friends, her marriage ended, and her dream of having a son was put on hold. The divorce was extremely hard on her and the girls. One day, she went from being a wife and a helper to being a single parent and primary provider for her family. Her dream of having a son one day was slipping further away with each passing day. My friend is a beautiful woman—both inside and out. But the characteristic that I love most about her is that she loves children. Actually, that was one of the many things that drew me to her. She loves children and children love her. We attended the same church, and we both worked in the children's ministry for many years. She is just a good person and an excellent mother. She practically raised her girls single-handedly after her husband left. They meant everything to her. And although she suffered tremendous emotional and financial hardships for many years, she never gave up on her dream to have a son. She was convinced that one day, God would make her whole.

She dreamed of getting married again, but this time, she wanted the marriage to last forever. This woman was no stranger to disappointments and pain. She has had her heart broken time and time again. I remember one time she was dating an old schoolmate of mine. They met in a Bible study group that I ran in my home for seven years. At first, we were sure that this man could very well be the husband that she had been praying for, but we were both wrong. The breakup was bitter, and it broke her heart again. One Wednesday night in church, God spoke to me and told me to tell her that He had heard her prayers and that He was going to give her the son that she had been praying for. But that wasn't all that God told me. He told me that He was going to give her more children. I heard the voice of God so clearly, almost as if He was sitting right next to me in the pew. I had heard right—more children even though she had only prayed for a son. I still remember the look on her face when I said, "More children." She laughed and said, "Children, I'll just settle for one just as long as it's a boy."

We both held on to the promise for years but nothing happened. Years went by, but no husband and no more children. There were times—many times—when I doubted myself. But I knew in my heart that it was God that had spoken to me that night in church. I was certain of it! Years later, she finally met, fell in love, and married a wonderful man with two children of his own—a son and a daughter. This wonderful man is my brother, Peter. He had just lost his girlfriend, who was the mother of one of his children—a son. My nephew was quite young when his mother died. After her death, Peter lost himself. He started to disappear slowly right in front of our eyes, and we didn't know how to help him. He took some time off from work, which helped a great deal, but he was in a lot of pain. The pain and grief from losing the love of his life was consuming him slowly.

One day, I was at the hairdresser with my two sisters, Rose and Joan, and I was telling them how concerned I was about my friend, Beverly. I told them how we had been praying for God to send her a husband and how lonely she was. The three of us started brainstorming about whom we knew and who would be a good man to set up with my friend. All of a sudden, my sister Joan said, "The only good man I know and he's single is Peter." It was as if a light went on in my head. *That's it,* I thought. *They would be perfect for each other.* I didn't let on to my sisters what I was up to because it's not always a good thing to play matchmaker, especially if it doesn't work.

As soon as I got home, I called my brother first and asked him if he was ready to start dating again. Honestly, I don't believe he was, but when I told him who I had in mind, he agreed. As soon as I hung up the telephone from talking to Peter, I called Beverly and asked her if she would like to go out with my one of my brothers. I had to tell her which one because I have a lot of brothers. (That's a long story) Because she already knew Peter and thought that he was handsome, and he is, she also agreed. The both of them hit it off on the first date. After that, they were inseparable. Within a year, they were married. They were like the Brady bunch on the old television series. They built a brand-new house, and Beverly and her three girls and Peter and his son moved in. Not long afterwards, Beverly became pregnant and had a son, Tristan. She was living her dream—it had finally come true. The wonderful husband, the brand-new house, and now, a beautiful baby boy, but God had another surprise for her. One that would change her relationship with God forever! About a year after she had her miracle baby boy, I had a dream that she had another son. This child looked almost identical to the other boy—just a little younger.

The very next day after I had the dream, I went over to their house for a visit, and we got to talking. I felt an impression in my heart to tell her about the dream that I had the night before about her having another baby boy. And lo and behold, she just started laughing hysterically. Apparently, she and her husband had just decided the night before that they wanted to have another baby, and there I was telling her that I had already seen it in a dream. I had the dream the same night they decided to try again. My dream was a confirmation that God had another son for them. Wasn't it incredible how God not only wanted to give her one son, but two? That's what you call double for your trouble. A year later, they had another baby boy. Between the two of them, they have seven children. This is what God will do if you dare to dream big. Take the limits off of God and He will give you exceedingly, abundantly above all that we ask or think. Now, can you see why my friend reminded me so much of President Abraham Lincoln? She never gave up her dream even though she had two miscarriages in the process.

Dare to Dream Big!

There's a program on television called *America's Next Top Model*. I have been watching it for the past couple of months, and although I had never dreamed of being a model, I like the show. Every week, they would eliminate one contestant with the intention of choosing a winner in the end. The show is produced by ex-supermodel Tyra Banks, who is also one of the judges. The panel consisted of distinguished judges, all experts in their field—fashion! They judge young women from different nationalities and background competing for their lifelong dream of becoming a supermodel like their illustrious host. The judges don't just look for outer beauty but also for inner. They are looking for personality, confidence, charisma, etc., but most of all, something that sets that person apart from the rest—that "it" factor.

In one of the seasons, there was a young girl that was odd. She was over six feet tall, and that was a rare thing for a fashion model. And to top it off, she was clumsy and awkward, nothing like the other girls. And if those weren't bad enough, she was shy. All the other girls didn't like her. They never took her seriously. She didn't pose a real threat to any of them because she stuck out like a sore thumb! Week after week, this plain, ordinary, shrinking violet blossomed among roses and lilies and other beautiful exotic flowers from all over the United States of America. Week after week, she survived the eliminations, which shocked the other contestants. None of them understood why this girl was still in the running. To the naked eye, she looked like coal, but the judges saw more! They saw a diamond in the ruff. She kept advancing while the more beautiful, confident, outgoing girls were being eliminated one by one. This ordinary, lanky, plain Jane went all the way to the end and won! Even she was blown away by her victory.

When she gave her victory speech, she humbly confessed that she never thought in a million years that she would have won. When asked why she had bothered to enter the competition if she thought that she couldn't win, she said, "I had a dream and I had to try." She was the ultimate underdog, if I ever saw one. But her victory rekindled a fire in my soul about my own lost dreams mangled and swept away by delays and disappointments over the years. Dreams that I thought were dead, suddenly, came back to life. This girl's dream came to pass because she dared to dream, and she dared to dream what seemed like an impossible dream. The Bible says in First Corinthians 1:27, "But God has chosen the foolish things of the world to put to shame the wise, and God has chosen the weak things of the world to put to shame the things which are mighty." God used the television program to encourage me that He and He alone always have the last word!

When God Speaks

Two years ago, when my daughter was still in college, she called me up one night, and she was deeply disturbed about a relationship she was in and where it was heading. At that time, she was dating this young man for about two years, but the relationship wasn't going anywhere. They were arguing a lot, and the stress from the relationship was interfering with her studies. Although they were both attending the same college and had been dating on and off since they were kids, something was definitely putting a strain on the relationship. My daughter wanted to know if she was wasting her time trying to hang on to a relationship that God was trying to pull apart. At that time, I too was at a crossroad in my life and had a very important decision to make. I was torn. That night, my daughter and I prayed together on the telephone and ask God to give us the answers that we needed in a dream.

That same night, we both had a dream, and God answered our prayers. God showed my daughter that the relationship wasn't going anywhere and that it was going to end. She was livid when she called me the next day and told me about her dream. In my dream, it was the opposite. God told me that He was going to restore a friendship that had been lost for many years, but I didn't want to hear that. The truth of the matter was I didn't want to reconcile with this person. The trust had been broken and I didn't want to open up myself to getting hurt again. We were both unhappy with our answers, but we knew that our dreams were from God. Now—only two years later—my daughter and her boyfriend are no longer together, and she has been trying to move on. But I am still resisting reconciliation even though this person wants to reconcile. I'm certain that God has already spoken and the answer was clear, but to be perfectly honest with you—I'm afraid!

A beautiful Christian woman once told me, "God will never take you anywhere His grace won't keep you." Even though I know in my heart of hearts that if reconciliation isn't the right thing for me, then God would have said no so why am I so afraid? Nevertheless, I know that I have to be obedient and, at least, try to reach out to this person. The Bible said that obedience is better than sacrifices. In other words, if you don't listen and obey, there will be consequences. I don't want to look back one day and wonder what God had in mind and what might have been. I don't want to lose out on a blessing, like the couple that had decided not to go back one more time to have the baby boy that they desperately wanted. Whether they thought that they were too old to start over with an infant or maybe they were afraid that they would get another girl and be disappointed again or there were other mitigating circumstances that nobody knows about. My problem is, I don't want to wake up one day and realize that I made the same mistake they did. It's funny how I was certain that God would have said yes to my daughter's question and no to mine. But God has His reasons why He doesn't grant every prayer request. We may not understand the reasoning behind His decisions, but in the light of future developments, we usually do.

Understanding Your Dreams

Dreams can be complicated and understanding them can be even more. When trying to understand your dreams, you must pray and ask God for the interpretation, especially before you act on them. The meanings of dreams are often symbolic. Very seldom are they actually literal. What one symbol represents in one person's dream may not be the same in another. Just as how we are individually unique to God, so are the ways He communicates to us. In my case, God usually talks to me in my dreams—literally. For instance, two years ago, I had a dream that my son Jordan won the Rookie of the Year award in basketball. Guess what? My son won the Rookie of the Year award, in his freshman year, in college. It doesn't get any plainer than that.

Several years ago, I had another dream that I was getting married. I have heard that a wedding in a dream represent the opposite—death! In my dreams, a wedding is a wedding. I dreamed that it was my wedding day, and I was in my bedroom getting dressed and chatting away with my sister Rose, who was my maid of honor. I was seated on a stool in front of a beautiful old antique dresser, putting on my makeup in front of the mirror. Out of the blue, my sister said the strangest thing to me. She said, "You've been waiting for this day for a very long time. How does it feel?" I started crying. I was so overwhelmed with emotions that I didn't even answer her.

To this day, years later, I can still feel the emotions that I felt in the dream that night. Since I was already married in reality, I didn't have a clue why I had dreamed that I was getting married. So I dismissed the dream, at the time, as being a natural dream, only to find out years later that it was in fact a spiritual dream. On December 31, 2008, that dream came to pass when my husband and I renewed our vows on our twenty-fifth wedding anniversary. On the morning of the wedding, I was sitting on a stool in front of a beautiful old antique dresser, putting on my makeup in front of the mirror. It happened exactly the way I had seen it in my dream years before. I was even talking to my sister Rose, who was, in fact, my maid of honor, both in my dream and in reality.

Although most of my dreams are literal, occasionally, God talks to me in symbols, like a dream that I had in 2006. I dreamed that I had two beautiful baby girls—identical twins and one of them died! In my dream, I had just put down one of the babies in her crib for a nap and was standing in the kitchen with the other one in my arms, fixing a bottle for her. The baby just made a sudden jerk as if something had startled her, and she fell out of my arms unto the ceramic tile floor. I was wearing high-heel shoes and accidentally stepped on my baby's head. Her head exploded like a watermelon all over the kitchen floor. I can still remember the popping sound it made, like a balloon bursting. I screamed so loudly that I woke up in a cold sweat screaming my head off. My scream woke up my husband instantly. He thought that I was having a heart attack or something.

I had the dream on a Friday night. I remember it vividly because I went to bed troubled in my spirit that night. We were selling our house, and it had been on the market for a couple of months, but we weren't getting any offers on it—maybe just one. After we listed our house for sale, three more houses on our street went up for sale, and they all sold before ours. I was discouraged and confused. That Friday night after my husband came home from work, I told him that I was having second thoughts about selling our house and, maybe, we should reconsider. My husband asks me to take the weekend and pray about it, and if I still felt the say way on Monday, then we should take the house off the market.

I prayed earnestly and asked God to tell me what to do because I didn't want to make the wrong decision. When I got the dream, I knew that it was the answer, but the dream was symbolic, and I'm not very good at reading symbols. The next day, all day, I was perturbed about the dream. I told my husband about it, but he didn't have a clue what it meant. Later that afternoon, my sister Rose came by, and I told her about the dream.

She told me to pray and ask God for the interpretation, and I did. The following day, on the Monday morning, God revealed the answer to me. Remember my husband gave me until Monday to decide what I wanted to do about the house? To make a long story short, the two babies, identical girls, represented two houses—the one was that we were going to sell and the other house that we were planning to buy afterward. The baby that fell out of my arms represented the house that I was selling and my decision to take it off the market. God was telling us that it would be a mistake to not sell it. We trusted what we felt God was saying to us, and we made the decision to stay the course. Within a week, the house was sold, and we used the money from the sale of that house to build a brand-new house.

Had we not heeded the warning from the dream, we would have changed our minds and taken the house off the market. I had allowed discouragement to set in because the house was taking too long to sell. Sometimes when we are waiting on God to answer our prayers and He's taking too long, we are tempted to give up in despair and quit! Quitting is not an option; it's a cop-out. If we are to receive anything from God, we have to wait patiently for the answer. But when God finally speaks, you will know it. You might be saying right now, "No, I don't always know when God is speaking to me. It's not that simple." I didn't say it was. God knows how to get our attention. He created us, and He knows how our minds work.

Understanding symbols can be complicated. I still don't understand a lot of them even after all these years. For example, babies. Babies in a dream always represent something good, like a dream or a goal—something that the dreamer really wants. And sometimes, it could even be an actual baby—if that's what the dreamer desires. Water—whenever I dream about water, especially if I am submerged in it, it usually means problems or depression. Years ago, I had a dream about my daughter, Shea-Marie, being submerged in water. In my dream, someone tied her hands and feet, placed her in a garbage bag, and tied the mouth of the bag with a rope. Then she was thrown into a large body of water, like an ocean. I dove into the water looking for her, but I couldn't find her.

After several unsuccessful dives, I was exhausted, but I couldn't quit. She was my daughter, my baby girl. She was in trouble, and I had to do whatever I could to save her. I kept diving again and again, deeper and deeper with each dive, until I saw an object way off in the distance. At first sight, it appeared to be a garbage bag, but I wasn't sure. But when I approached the object, it became clearer. And soon, I realized that it was a garbage bag—the one that my daughter was encased in. I grabbed it and started ripping it apart as fast as I could because I was running out of air. I finally got it open, and there she was, all tied up with ropes—almost like a mummy. She was unconscious. She appeared to be dead! I picked her up and started swimming toward the surface. I was struggling under the deadweight of her lifeless body. I couldn't carry her for too much longer. I felt exhausted—my body was numb from the icy cold water. I started to sink slowly back into the bottomless sea. I was drowning on the verge of unconsciousness. We were both dying with no one to save either one of us.

Suddenly, I felt these huge pair of hands underneath me, pushing us up to the surface. I was carrying my daughter in my arms, and someone or something was carrying me. Whatever it was, human or God, thrust us with tremendous force out of the water and unto the shore. My daughter was still motionless—her hands and feet were still bound. I untied her and cradled her frozen body in my arms. I was weeping uncontrollably, thinking that she was dead, until she started coughing and water spewed out of her mouth. She opened up her eyes and took a deep breath. She was alive! We were both alive, but I wasn't the savior; something greater than ourselves, a higher power, intervened and saved our lives.

The next morning, after I woke up, I didn't need a crystal ball to tell me the meaning of my dream. At that time, in both of our lives, my daughter and I were going through a lot of troubles. My daughter had just finished high school, and her applications to the dental hygiene program to five different colleges were rejected. She had always dreamed of becoming a dental hygienist since she was old enough to hold a toothbrush. When she didn't get into college and then she broke up with her boyfriend, she went into a depression. I did everything within my power to help her, but she kept spiraling deeper and deeper into this dense fog. I was genuinely afraid for her life because she was in a lot of pain, and I was concerned as to what she might do.

After I had the dream, I knew that God was warning me about the severity of her pain and the state of mind that she was in. I knew the water, in my dream, represented all the pain and grief that she and I were both engulfed in. The garbage bag represented how my daughter felt when her boyfriend ended their relationship after two and a half years. It broke her heart. She felt like her boyfriend had thrown her away like garbage. She felt rejected and unworthy. As for me, even though I was going through my own problems, God used me to help my daughter and then turned around and delivered me out of my own troubles. In the end, God saved us both just like in the dream!

CHAPTER 5

Disappointments

Oliver Wendell Holmes said, "If I had a formula for bypassing trouble, I wouldn't pass it around. I wouldn't be doing anyone a favor. Trouble creates a capacity to handle it . . . Meet it as a friend, for you'll see a lot of it and you had better be on speaking terms with it."

Stranded at the Airport

The word "disappoint" means "to fail to meet the expectation or hope." Every single person on this planet has gone through disappointments and has had their heart broken countless times. Disappointments are a vital part of the human experience. It's inevitable! How we deal with them is crucial. Some lessons in life can only be understood through disappointments and troubles. One of the many mysteries of God's nature is to allow unspeakable, unexplainable pain and suffering to happen to His children.

Our human mind cannot fathom that. We can't imagine doing or even allowing bad things to happen to our loved ones! So when God does, it confuses us. We think that He's cruel and He doesn't really love us—but it's not true! Unfortunately, some of the most important lessons that God wants to teach us is best learned during the most painful circumstances of our lives. God wants to teach us how to respond to pain differently. If I live to be a hundred years old, and I believe I will, there wouldn't be enough time to tell you all the times I felt like God had disappointed me. With the exceptions of all the miscarriages I have suffered, the stories that

I'm about to share with you in this chapter are some of the most illogical disappointments ever.

On December 3, 2008, my husband and I celebrated twenty-five years of marriage. I hadn't planned on doing anything more than a romantic candlelight dinner for two, with a bottle of my favorite wine, and maybe a movie, if either one of us can stay awake long enough to watch it. But when my sister Rose asked me what I was planning on doing and I told her, she encouraged me to change my plans and do something a bit more memorable. You see, my sister had just recently lost her husband of twenty-four years to cancer in 2005. That year, 2007, they would have celebrated their twenty-fifth wedding anniversary, if he had lived. I told her that I would give some serious thoughts to what she had said and I would pray about it.

I finally came up with something special to memorialize the occasion. When I told my sister what I had in mind, she loved it. I had decided to renew my wedding vows on a five-day cruise to the Bahamas. Since my anniversary was in December, I thought that a Christmas cruise with all the trimmings would be spectacular! I had envisioned a large formal Christmas ceremony on board a cruise ship with my family and friends. I couldn't wait to announce my intentions at Christmas dinner at Rose's house, which was exactly one year before the blessed event. I wanted to give everyone sufficient time to come up with their money. I had already enlisted the professional services of a travel agent, who was a childhood friend, and asked her to coordinate the travel portion. My niece volunteered to be my wedding planner at home, and since she was an event planner by profession, I was more than happy to solicit her services. The cruise cost $1,500 per person, and we were required to make our payments in three installments with the final payment due two months before departure.

Forty-two of my family and friends signed on for the cruise of a lifetime! My immediate family, which included five of us, was the largest. That makes five of us at $1,500 per person. I needed to come up with $7,500 plus the cost of the wedding package that the cruise ship was offering. When I came up with the idea to renew my vows, I had no money. My two children were in college, and I had tuition payments and mortgage payments coming out of my eyeballs. Furthermore, we had just built a house in Jamaica that same year, in 2008, so money was tight! But I had my heart set on a fairly large wedding party, especially since I had only one girl in my wedding party twenty-five years ago.

I had always dreamed of having a Cinderella wedding ever since I was a little girl, and my dream was finally coming true. I settled on four girls and four guys, not including, the bride and groom. The initial deposit, which was the most important payment, holds your spot on the cruise. That payment was only $25 per person, and it was due in February 2008, two months after I made the announcement. All forty-two people handed in their money, and I was pleasantly surprised at the large number of people who had seriously expressed an interest into going. In my experience, I knew that money talks, so I was prepared that we were going to lose some. By the time the second deposit came due, which was in August, for $200 per person, we had lost twelve people—leaving thirty. I was still happy with that number. It was already September, and we were getting close to the final deadline to pay off the balance. I needed $6,375 by the end of October and I didn't have it. I had been praying for almost a year for God to bring in the money before October, but it was already September and no money.

I remember being at the hairdresser's early one Saturday morning in September. The hair salon opens at 8:00 a.m. on Saturday mornings, and usually, I am the first one through the doors. I was sitting in the chair—praying—while my hairdresser was cutting my hair. I told God that I needed Him to come through for me in a mighty way because it would be such a huge embarrassment to plan such an elaborate wedding when I knew we couldn't afford it. I had asked God to work a financial miracle on my behalf, and to my surprise, after I got home that afternoon, my husband told me that he had miraculously come into a lot of money. I was dumbfounded! I didn't believe him for a good hour or more before he finally convinced me that he was telling the truth.

At first, I thought that he was joking because my husband has a great sense of humor. But he wasn't! God gave us more than enough money to pay off the balance on the cruise with extra money to spare. The money came in only a couple of weeks before the deadline even though I had been praying for almost a year. I was the first one to pay off my balance even though my bill was the largest. God not only gave me enough money to pay for the cruise and wedding package that I had chosen but He also gave my husband enough money to buy the beautiful diamond ring I had my eye on. And to top it off, the local newspaper picked up our story, and we became local celebrities virtually overnight. Everywhere we went, in the bank, in the grocery store, in the gym, people would approach us and tell us how inspired they were by the article.

Heart of Gold

The heartfelt details of the article went as follows:

Heart of Gold

Raffleton Dixon knew he had a heart as big as a Bob Marley hit tune. He just needed to show Althea Lee. And that wasn't easy—at first. Althea, 21, was standing outside a Kitchener house party when Raffleton, who's known to his friends as Dixon, walked in. Dixon, 22, was a high-energy DJ from Hamilton; a rapper with a powerful sound system and a vast collection of records.

They didn't speak then. But more than 25 years later; Dixon remembers how beautiful she was, and what she was wearing. A month later, the two met at another party. Dixon asked Althea to dance. Althea remembered the DJ. She wasn't enthusiastic.

"I didn't like him then," she says. "I didn't like what he was saying . . . the rapping, some of his lyrics." "That DJ wasn't me; it was my twin brother;" said Dixon, pulling her leg. They danced, and he drove her home.

It was a hit-and-miss kind of a relationship in the beginning though Althea, a Conestoga College student then, was trying her darndest not to make it a relationship at all. One night, Althea was looking for a way to say goodbye when Dixon took her aside. His words surprised her.

"I'm not good-looking," Dixon told her, "but I have a good heart." "That's how I felt at the time," Dixon says today. "I know I have a good heart. Nobody knows me but me."

Althea took another look. Every day, she's glad she did. Because she married the kind of man who will work two jobs every day to support his family. Who will drive, at the end of a long day, to London to pick up their college student son who missed the bus home. Who will sell his cherished record collection—Bob Marley, Burning Spear, Johnny Mathis, and more—to pay the first year college tuition for their daughter.

Who never turns down a relative in need because quite simply "we are family"? Who puts a record on the turntable and dances with her in the kitchen of their gracious Kitchener home. "She's my heartbeat," he says. "He's beautiful, inside and out," Althea says. "My life with him is like breathing. It's just natural . . . He makes you feel like you're worth it. You're valuable."

They came from the same country but different worlds. Both immigrated to Canada from Jamaica, where Althea's middle-class family lived in the city. Dixon's family was poor and lived in the country. Dixon was 15 when his mother, who came to Canada to work as a nanny, sent for him and five siblings. His mother, now deceased, would tell Althea how Dixon, as a little boy in Jamaica, would fetch her at night from the sugarcane field where she was working.

He carried a torch to light their way. "She'd see a little light in the dark and she'd know it was Raffleton coming to find her." In Canada, Dixon worked in record shops and factories to save enough money for a car and DJ equipment. He was a good DJ. But "when the kids came along, I had to walk away from that," he says. "It's hectic and can be violent." There wasn't much money when they decided to marry. Dixon bought a $50 engagement ring, vowing one day to replace it. They married December 3, 1983.

For the past 19 years, Dixon has worked full time for a pipe company in Guelph. He starts at 4 a.m. and works until noon. Then he snatches a few hours' sleep and starts his part-time job with a courier company. He has done both jobs for the last eight years. "We didn't have much growing up," Dixon says. "I felt if I grow up and have a family, I want to do whatever it takes to take care of my family."

Today, the couple's daughter Shea-Marie, 21, and son Jordan, 19, are in college. Philip is 11. "I don't want them to work as hard as I do," says Dixon, who left school after Grade 11 to help his mother. "If they get an education, they'll be better off." His children's happiness means everything. "When I come home and hear them laughing upstairs, that's the best time." There have been tears, as well. In 1988, the couple lost twin boys who died soon after they were born prematurely.

"It was devastating for us," Althea says. "But we took the good and the bad and we make it work." Next month, 30 family and friends will honor the couple whose home is always open to them. They've saved their money to accompany the couple on a five-day cruise, Althea, 49, and Dixon, 50, will renew their wedding vows. Dixon will give her a beautiful new ring as he promised 25 years ago. Althea will give him a pendant in the shape of the North Star, which suits him, she says. "My husband is constant in our marriage. He's as steady as a rock. He's always there when you need him." A DJ will play their wedding song, Johnny Mathis's "Misty," and they'll dance.

The excitement leading up to the wedding was electrifying. I elected to wear a sexy long, form-fitted, slinky, fuchsia wedding dress with a low-cut back and fuchsia stilettos. I was smoking hot!!! The girls wore beautiful silver dresses with matching silver shoes—befitting a silver wedding anniversary ceremony. My husband wore a silver gray suit with white shirt, and the groomsmen all wore black suits with silver shirts and silver and black ties. It ended up being a picture-perfect wedding, but unfortunately, it didn't start out that way. We were supposed to sail on December 27, 2008, and my wedding was scheduled for the next day—December 28. Our party of thirty got split up into three groups, all of us travelling on three separate airplanes. My immediate family of five, along with thirteen others, was scheduled to fly out last. The others went with Delta Airlines and got off to a good start.

Our group of eighteen was flying with United Airlines from Toronto, Canada, to Washington, D.C., and on to Jacksonville—where we were scheduled to sail from. The eighteen of us were like little children at the fair. It was exhilarating! We all met at the airport, went as far as boarding the aircraft, and then the plane broke down on the runway. We were asked to deplane and wait inside the terminal for further instructions. After a while, it was clear that we weren't going anywhere for some time. The announcement finally came, and it wasn't what we had hoped for. Our airplane was grounded, and because our party was so large in number, and it being Christmas time, all flights were booked solid for the next two days.

Therefore, United Airlines offered to put us up in a nearby hotel for two days and we were rebooked on another flight. Unfortunately, because we had to board the ship at Jacksonville that same day, we missed the ship. The captain of the ship offered to reschedule our wedding ceremony if we were able to catch up with the ship in Freeport, Bahamas. All eighteen of us chased the ship for three days before we caught up with it. Our group was eventually split up into two, and my immediate family of five was the last to board the ship. By the time we boarded, most of us, including myself, were sick with the flu. All I wanted to do was to sleep for a long time. I was exhausted! Upon arrival, we were met by everyone including the others that flew with Delta Airlines. You could see the look of disappointment and relief upon their faces. Just try to imagine being invited to a wedding and the bride and groom didn't show up. The only good thing to come out of that entire ordeal was how kind the captain and crew members were toward us.

The captain had given instructions to my wedding coordinator on board the ship to book my wedding on whatever day I wanted and to do whatever she could to help make my wedding day memorable. My friend Ann, the travel agent that booked the entire cruise for me, made arrangements to have my cabin beautifully decorated in my wedding colors—silver and fuchsia. When my husband and I opened the door to our cabin, we were speechless! We ordered room service and crashed for the night. The next morning, I met with the wedding planner, and we put together the most breathtaking wedding ceremony ever!

Because the captain had told my wedding coordinator to give me anything I wanted, I upgraded my wedding package to something more elaborate! All in all, we were able to salvage two out of five days and renewed our vows as planned. God answered my prayer and gave me a wedding that was unforgettable! And I mean that literally! Looking back at everything that happened, I often wondered why God didn't put us on another flight or arranged a rescue flight to get us to our destination. That's what most reputable airlines would have done.

We were extremely dissatisfied with United Airlines and Carnival Cruise Lines to the point where we all wrote letters to the president of both companies in hopes that they would have done more to make us whole, but they didn't. They didn't offer us anything, not even travel vouchers or, at least, another cruise of a lesser value. Taking into consideration that the trip was to commemorate our twenty-fifth wedding anniversary and the hell that the eighteen of us, including children, had to endure, we thought that United Airlines and Carnival Cruise Lines would have been more sympathetic. My mother, seventy-three years old at the time, became very ill upon returning home to Canada. But that didn't move United Airlines and Carnival Cruise Lines one bit. To say that I wasn't disappointed with God with the way things turned out would be a lie. It was a major letdown just like the next story I'm about to share with you, but this disappointment had nothing to do with my Heavenly Father. This one was all about my earthly father.

The Wedding Dress

This story is one of the reasons why I made the decision to renew my vows on my twenty-fifth wedding anniversary. As I had mentioned before, I had a small wedding ceremony in the middle of winter, but I didn't have a choice. Money was tight, but we had planned a small formal ceremony that blew up in our faces. My father had promised to purchase my wedding dress as a gift to me. I had always dreamed of having the long white Cinderella wedding dress that most little girls dream about from childhood. So you can just imagine how happy I was when my father agreed to pay for my dress because I knew that I couldn't afford it.

I couldn't wait to hit the bridal stores for the perfect dress. The very first store, The Bridal Penthouse, had my Cinderella dress—it was stunning! It was the dress of my dreams, and it was mine—so I thought. I told my father about the dress, and he told me to go ahead and order it into my size. The dress cost $500, and in 1983, that was expensive. So you can just imagine how exquisite it was. It took about six to eight weeks before my dress finally arrived from Montreal. As soon as I received the telephone call that my dress had come in, I told my father.

I couldn't believe my ears when my father told me that he wasn't going to pay for my dress. His exact words were "Where do you expect me to get the money from?" I almost had a heart attack when I heard what he said. He insisted that he couldn't afford to pay for the dress and that I should return it. I knew that he wasn't telling me the truth because my father owned and operated a successful construction company for many years. He had the money, but because he was about to walk out on his wife and children right after he walked me down the aisle, he wasn't about to invest $500 into the biggest day of my entire life. I cried for a very long time over the disappointment of returning that dress. And it took me even longer to forgive my father for reneging on his promise. Because money was an issue, a limited issue for my fiancé and I, I ended up buying a cocktail dress for less than $100, but it was beautiful.

It was such a huge emotional disappointment for me that it took many years before I confronted my father and told him how much his actions, or should I say lack thereof, hurt me. Conveniently for him, he claimed that he didn't remember any of it, but he did apologize, and I accepted. Not all of our disappointments are orchestrated by God. But as His children, one of the most common misconceptions that we have about God is that we expect Him to protect us from pain. We believe that God is supposed to act and think like earthly parents. We think that because we would do anything within our power to help and protect our children, we expect God to do the same for us. We believe that because God can see sickness, pain, death, and hardships before they come upon us, we expect him to divert them and not to allow bad things to happen to us if He truly love and care for us. And when He doesn't, we get angry with God and turn away from Him.

I am the first to admit that I don't understand God and most likely never will. I get just as confused and disoriented when bad things happen to me and to my family. And I would be the biggest liar in the world if I didn't admit that there were times in my life when I never thought that I would ever put my trust in God again. My husband is the complete opposite of me. He believes that if you want something, then you have to go out and make it happen. I can count on both hands how many times in the past thirty years I have actually seen my husband on his knees praying or see him reading a book, including the Bible.

Yet, I am constantly on my knees praying, and I am always reading a book, especially my Bible. I seriously doubt if my husband will ever read this book. I remember asking him once why I had never seen him on his knees praying or reading the Bible. He told me that I did enough praying and reading for the both of us only to watch me endure one disappointment after another. He also admitted that he didn't want to set up himself to be disappointed like I had. He was right. I am a dreamer, and a true dreamer never ever stops dreaming. Unfortunately, I can write another book filled with stories about all the times God has disappointed me throughout my life. But I could also write many books filled with stories about His goodness and mercy toward me.

God wants to show me how to relinquish all my disappointments into His capable hands and trust Him to redeem the losses. Now, every time God doesn't answer my prayers the way I think He should, I just go after Him with everything I've got. When I need something from God, I don't quit asking. I'm like a pit bull. When I sink my teeth into something, I hold on for dear life! Have you ever noticed the wide jaws on a pit bull? That's what makes that particular breed of dogs dangerous. Once they lock down on something, it's virtually impossible to pry their jaws loose. This is the best way I can explain how I am when I stand in faith with God. I never give up! I never ever surrender—even if I get beaten to a pulp. A Creator who has the power and wisdom to create everything out of nothing is great enough to be trusted with my disappointments and failures. I may not understand God, but this one thing I know—I love Him with all of my heart and soul.

My Mother-in-law's Death

I think that when my husband lost his mother to cancer in 1998, it really did a number on him. By then, we had suffered so many losses as a young couple, he just stopped believing. He was disappointed with God! My mother-in-law was one of those people who suffered greatly! On June 18, 1998, she lost her battle to ovarian cancer at the age of sixty-seven. Nobody knew that she was ill—not even her. That's the thing about this type of cancer. By the time you start exhibiting symptoms, most often, it's too late! She had just retired two years prior and was getting ready to reap the fruits of her labor. She had always been in good health, never been sick a day in her life. Worked two jobs for many years and single-handedly raised seven children alone.

She migrated to Canada in 1968, worked as a nanny originally, and sent for six of her seven children. The eldest, a son, was an adult and was living on his own at that time. He chose to stay behind to be with his girlfriend and their children. She eventually built a house in Jamaica with the intention of going back one day to enjoy her retirement years in the sunshine. But unfortunately, that didn't happen. One day, she just wasn't feeling like her energetic, bubbly self—that's what she was like. Always on the go, helping her children and grandchildren in whatever way she could. She was complaining about a pain that she had in her side. "It just suddenly came out of nowhere," she said.

At first, she brushed it off as a strained muscle from when she was vacuuming her apartment a couple of days earlier, but after she tried to pick up my baby and belted out a scream, we knew it was more than just a strained muscle. My son Philip was only ten months old, so he wasn't that heavy for her to react that way. We urged her to go to the doctor the next day and have it checked out. She went the next day as she had promised, and her family doctor sent her straight to the emergency room after he examined her. They admitted her, and she never left the hospital alive. She was diagnosed with advanced ovarian cancer and died two weeks later. All the prayers in the world didn't save her life. It was just her time to die.

As a matter of fact, she suffered! She was in so much pain that my husband couldn't stand to watch her suffer anymore. One night, after we got home from visiting her at the hospital, he wept! He was in so much pain watching her fade away slowly before our eyes. Feeling totally impotent, not being able to do something—anything—to end her suffering. He asked me to pray with him that God would take her that same night. That was one of the few times in our marriage that I ever saw my husband on his knees. Guess what? My mother-in-law died the very next day. We went to the hospital the next evening, and as we were walking past the nurses' station, one of the nurses stopped us and told us the good news. My mother-in-law had just died only twenty minutes before we arrived.

When we entered her room, the expression of peace that was upon her face was indescribable! It was as if she had been ready to leave this chapter of her life behind to start a new one. I watched my husband as he stood by her bed side and gently touched her face. I heard him talking to her quietly underneath his breath, but I couldn't hear what he was saying. After we left the hospital and went home, he told me that when he touched his mother's face, she was still warm to the touch. Apparently, that meant a lot to him somehow. Although he was disappointed with God for not sparing his mother's life, he felt grateful that, at least, her suffering was over.

I heard an interesting story about death that helped me to grasp a better revelation of what happens when we die. When a little boy that was dying of heart failure asked his doctor about God and why God was taking him so early, the doctor said the strangest thing to him. He told the little boy that God wasn't taking him to heaven; He was just receiving him. I never thought about death that way before, but I liked that explanation.

Fiftieth Birthday Disaster!

On May 11, 2009, I celebrated my fiftieth birthday. This was only six months after my twenty-fifth wedding anniversary cruise disaster. I thought that since my wedding anniversary didn't happen quite the way I had anticipated, maybe I should do something special to celebrate my fiftieth birthday. I had always planned on doing something significant for my fiftieth birthday anyway, but I never really knew what I wanted to do—only that it would be significant, something that I would remember for the rest of my life. One day, my sister and I were driving back from the hairdresser, and she asked me what I had planned for my birthday. I told her that I was considering taking a trip but I hadn't figured out exactly where I wanted to go yet. She reminded me that I said that I had always wanted to visit Australia one day and urged me to consider taking the trip for my birthday. I thought about it for a while, spoke to my husband about it, and then finally settled on Australia. Once again, I contacted my friend Ann, the travel agent, and she advised me not to go to Australia in May.

Apparently, May in Australia is like autumn in Canada—it's cold! So I decided to wait until December, which would be summer in Australia.

We booked the trip for December 10, 2009, seven months after my actual birthday, but at least, the weather would be hot, and I love hot! We booked and paid for it months in advance. I chose a fancy hotel right downtown Sydney, Australia, and I just couldn't wait for December to arrive; until October 11, 2009, the unthinkable happened. I suffered a ruptured brain aneurysm and ended up in a coma. Two months before we were supposed to leave on my dream vacation, I almost died. I had to cancel the trip, and I never celebrated my fiftieth birthday as I had always dreamed of.

Once again, another dream vacation blew up in my face. What are the odds of the aneurysm rupturing only two months before I was supposed to leave for Australia, forcing me to cancel the trip? I'm sure that I must have had the aneurysm for a long time before it ruptured. Actually, I was exhibiting symptoms for about two years before it ruptured, but I didn't know that I was ill. Why couldn't I have gone on the trip and come back before it ruptured. It felt like history was repeating itself, and the same misfortune that I had when I planned my twenty-fifth wedding anniversary renewal of vows ceremony, one year in advance, only to watch it fall apart when the airplane broke down on the runway.

One disappointment after another, and to this day, I still don't understand why. The Bible said that I am to be thankful in everything, and the word "everything" means all things—good and bad. What if I had gone to Australia and the aneurysm had ruptured there, it would have been far worse than it rupturing here, at home, in Canada. And when the airplane broke down on the runway on my way to the Bahamas, I tried my best to be thankful that, at least, the airplane didn't break down in the sky and kill my entire family. But I would be a liar to pretend like I wasn't disappointed in both cases because I was. I had expected God to work everything out for my good, and it didn't happen. I was disappointed with God.

The Business Opportunity

This is another story when I felt like God had truly let me down. It was in 1991, two years after my son Jordan was born; we had to sell our house before the bank foreclosed. We had just purchased the house three years prior in 1988. It was the first house we had ever owned, and it had a lot of sentiments attached to it. Furthermore, I had hired a profession decorator to remodel it to our liking. You should have seen what she did with the nursery. It was awesome! She totally captured the concept that I had envisioned for our first home. My daughter was a year old when we bought the house, and I was five months pregnant with my second child. My daughter's room looked like something out of a storybook. Perfectly befitting for a little princess and that she was. After the remodeling was finished, I saw myself living there and raising a family for a very long time.

One day, one of my brothers, presented a business opportunity that sounded lucrative. It was a chance to break into the real estate market. At that time, it was a buyer's market, and the houses in the city where we lived in were selling like hot cakes. Since my brother was a contractor, we jumped at the chance to invest. We foolishly mortgaged our house in order to come up with the money to invest not knowing that the market was going to take a nosedive. We lost our investment forcing us to sell our house before the bank foreclosed on it. I remember the day when we got the letter from the bank informing us of their intentions. I was heartbroken! This was our home, and we had two babies. All the hard work and labor of love we had invested in our home was going to be enjoyed by strangers. To make matters worse, I had my mother living with us at that time. She occupied the lower level, and we were on the main floor. It meant that she had to move as well. I prayed for months when we first started spiraling into debt. We needed a financial miracle to pay up what we owed the bank and to get back on track, but no miracle came.

At that time, I used to suffer from nosebleeds whenever I was stressed. The day we received the foreclosure letter, I cried so hard that I bled profusely all over my clothes. It was pitiful to see a grown woman acting like a baby. I knew what to do. It wasn't like I hadn't faced hardship before. I was a devout Christian. I grew up in the church. I had proven God countless times before, and I knew that I could trust Him with my life. Once I came to my senses, I dried my face, called a realtor, and listed our house for sale. I called the same realtor that I had met in 1988 when we were renting the house where the twins had died.

We explained to her the urgency of the situation and that we had to sell before the bank foreclosed. She supported us in whatever way she could because time was of the essence. The first offer came in within days of the listing, and we accepted it. It was considerably lower than we would have liked, but the real estate market was plummeting fast, and we had to sell. We got enough to satisfy the bank, but in the process, we weren't made whole. We had to vacate quickly—leaving us practically homeless.

My sister Rose and her husband graciously took us in while we looked for a place of our own. We stayed there a couple of weeks before we ended up at my mother-in-law's house about ninety kilometers away. The commute to work was an unwanted burden thrust upon my husband—considering he had to drive over two hours daily to get back and forth to work. I thank God for my mother-in-law—God rest her soul—who lost her battle in 1998 to ovarian cancer. If she hadn't helped us, I don't know what we would have done. Those couple of months tested our marriage commitment tremendously. That's what trials will do. Trials are meant to make us better, not bitter. And thank God, we weren't bitter. Finally, we took possession of one of the houses that we bought when we went into business with my brother. My brother and his family were living in it, and they moved out. Since we were part owners, we took possession of it. We lived there for fourteen years before we sold it.

Why didn't God bring in the money to pay off what we owed the bank and save us the embarrassment of foreclosure? There's no denying that God allowed the house to be sold within days of the listing, but we didn't want to sell our home. We had a family! It was our home! That wasn't the outcome we had envisioned. Was God faithful or did He let us down? To this day, I still don't know. What I do know is that I must have gone back to that house a million times. For a couple of years, the new owners hadn't made any changes to the appearance. It was almost like time had stood still, and we were still the owners. We were happy there. The child that God gave me after the death of my twins was born in that house—now strangers walked the hallways of the house I once called home. This story certainly didn't end the way I had hoped because I lost my home. I was disappointed with God.

An Angel on the Airplane

In 2005, I spent an entire summer in Jamaica researching the real estate market. At that time, my husband and I had been talking about buying a house for our retirement. Although I was only forty-six and my husband, forty-seven years old, we thought that before we knew it, retirement would be breathing down the back of our necks and we weren't prepared. Most people don't plan for retirement when they are young. You just never think about getting old when you're young. We fool ourselves into thinking that we have all the time in the world to prepare for those golden years, but in fact, we don't! I, on the other hand, just got up one morning and told my husband that it was time for us to look ahead and plan for when our children are gone, and it's just us. I had envisioned a small, simple country-style house by the sea, with lots of fruit trees and a swing. I love swings. I had one when I was a little girl growing up in Jamaica. My dad made it for us by tying a rope on one of the branches of the mango tree in the backyard. I used to spend a lot of time on the swing daydreaming about who I was going to marry and how many children I was going to have.

I had already done my homework by talking to friends and family living in Jamaica about the real estate market. Based on the information I had received, I took the trip with the intention of finding our dream house. And once I found it, my husband would join me and we would buy it. Our budget was tight, seeing that we already had a mortgage and three children, but we were confident that we had the mind of the Lord in this matter. I searched the entire summer for my dream house until I was blue in the face, but I couldn't find it. I couldn't find anything I liked within our price range. Sure! I looked at a lot of houses, but they were expensive. After a while, I saw my dream fading away like flowers in the fall.

Discouragement was starting to set in, and just when I was about to pack up my dream in an old kit bag, my son Philip flew to Jamaica to be with me for a couple of weeks. He was a welcomed distraction—one that I desperately needed and I loved having the company. The loneliness from being separated from my husband and children was beginning to take its toll on me. So when my son expressed an interest to join me, I was overjoyed! It was like having a miniature version of my husband, and his presence was quite comforting, especially when Hurricane Dennis took us by surprise. He was my little man around the house, and his childlike faith was an inspiration to me when I felt like quitting.

Either one of us hadn't experienced a hurricane before. I had my ears glued to the radio and television stations as they gave us a blow-by-blow report of the hurricane. Everyone was making the necessary preparations for a hurricane except for Philip and I. We didn't have a clue what we needed—after all, this was the first time we had ever experienced a hurricane. Fortunately for us, one of my friends came by and took us to the hardware store to buy hurricane supplies. We stocked up on nonperishable foods, water, candles, flashlights, and more . . . Upon returning from the store, we barricaded ourselves indoors and waited.

My entire family back in Canada kept calling us every hour on the hour. They had learned about the hurricane all the way in Canada. It was all over the news. Philip and I wanted to see up close and personal the effects of a real live hurricane. We stayed on the veranda for as long as we could until the hurricane struck. It was supposed to hit land by midmorning on July 7, 2005, but it had been raining for a couple of days prior. The night before, on July 6, it rained cats and dogs all night. We watched the rain and winds batter everything in sight. Water flooded the streets, creating widespread flash flooding. Enormous trees caved under the pressure of winds approximately 115 mph, broken branches and debris was hurled on rooftops causing horrendous damages to homes and businesses. Cars floated in the streets, with or without passengers, as Hurricane Dennis ravaged the small island of Jamaica, causing $31.7 million in damages

During the night, Philip became sick and started running a fever. He was burning up, and I didn't know what to do. Miraculously, my cell phone was still operable, ringing frequently between my husband and children in Canada, and a couple of concerned locals checking up on us. I did everything imaginable to bring his temperature down, but the fever wouldn't break. Finally just before dawn, the fever broke, but the storm hadn't. We huddled together underneath the covers listening to the thunderous winds beating against the doors and windows. Neither one of us slept a wink that night; we were in the middle of a category four hurricane. The island of Jamaica got a good gully washing before the hurricane passed and the waters subsided. Everything was in shambles. We had no running water or electricity for three days. The only water we had were the ones that we had stored in the house. We had to eat nonperishable foods and stayed indoors until the cleanup was completed.

It was an unforgettable experience. Hurricane Dennis was a force to be reckoned with, but all in all, we came away from the entire ordeal—unscathed. When it was declared safe to move about the island, I took my son everywhere with me; we became inseparable after that. Jamaica was far removed from the life my son had become accustomed to in Canada. It was a cultural shock experience for both of us, but in spite of the hardship, Jamaica is a beautiful island. Philip was having so much fun exploring my roots and learning how to use a slingshot that one of my friends gave him. Up to that point, he didn't have a clue what a slingshot was. Once he realized that he could use it to shoot lizards, which we both hated, he spent most of his time playing target practice with every creepy-crawly critters he could find. By the end of his stay, we were heartbroken when he had to return home.

When it came time for me to go home, I was going home empty-handed. I still hadn't found my dream house, and I was disappointed. To make matters worse, my sister's husband was dying of cancer, and I had to return home before he died. I boarded the aircraft feeling like the biggest loser. What I had gone to Jamaica to accomplish, I hadn't. I had reached an all-time low, and I was going home defeated. I felt like I had wasted my time and money and had accomplished nothing. My brother Mario was travelling with me to Canada to attend my brother-in-law's funeral. And I was grateful for the travelling companion. I was seated in the middle seat between two men—my brother on my left and a total stranger on my right. I didn't want to talk to anyone. I just wanted to crawl under a rock and stay there.

My brother and the gentleman struck up a conversation during the meal service. They kept leaning forward conversing back and forth across me as if I wasn't there. As much as I tried my darndest to be polite, I think they knew that I was annoyed by my silence. After dinner, my brother fell asleep, and the silence was golden. All of a sudden, the gentleman on my right started telling me a story. I knew he wasn't inebriated because he hadn't had any alcohol with his meal. But out of the blue, he started telling me a story about a house that he wanted to buy in Jamaica. When he was a little boy, he would walk by this big, beautiful house every day to get to school. Vowing one day when he grew up, he would buy this house—his dream house.

He migrated to Canada when he was a young man, but every time he would return home for a visit, he would imagine himself the proud owner of that house. One year, he went back for a visit like he had done many times, but this time was different. To his surprise, his dream house was for sale. Stunned by his findings, he rushed out to the bank and secured a preapproved mortgage to buy his dream house after what had seemed like a lifelong fantasy. He was certain that he had it in the bag even without knowing what the inside of the house looked like. When he was ready to make his move by approaching the owners of the house, he was flabbergasted to find that the house was sold. After all the years of dreaming about owning his dream house, the fantasy had come to an end, and he was heartbroken. He was so close to finally getting what he had hungered for all his life, but it wasn't meant to be. He grieved the loss of his dream for a long time before he finally relinquished it into God's hands. He made it a point to tell me that he chose to come to terms with the will of God for his life and that he knew in his heart that God didn't want him to have the house. "But why wouldn't God want you to have the house? I asked. "I don't know, but I do know that it wasn't out of spite, but out of love," he replied. He spoke to me as if he was privy to my dilemma—and yet, I hadn't met this man before that.

As he spoke, I found myself fighting back the tears. It was as if he was speaking directly into my pain, and his words of comfort broke through the barriers of shame and disappointment that had enveloped me. He lifted his arm as if to tell me that it was OK to put my head upon his chest. I placed my head upon the chest of a complete stranger on an airplane filled with people and wept! I believe to this day that I was comforted by an angel on an airplane. An angel sent by God to minister hope. Normally, I would have never done something so absurd! There was something oddly compelling about this man, Rupert. That was his name. Was he an angel or just a kind stranger with psychic abilities? The Bible says in Hebrews 13:1-2, "Let brotherly love continue. Do not forget to entertain strangers, for by so doing some has unwittingly entertained angels."

I will never forget the feelings of disappointment and failure that sheathed my heart that day. Had it not been for Rupert, my angel, I would have given up in despair. Everything happens for a reason. When things don't work out the way we anticipate, it doesn't mean that we were wrong in the first place. It only means that God has a better plan. This happened in 2005. In 2007, only two years later, I returned to Jamaica to look at some houses that my father told me about. When I saw the model home, I was speechless.

It was exactly what I was looking for and affordable too. I didn't waste any time picking a lot, and one year later, in 2008, it was completely finished. Three years after I had encountered what I believed to be an angel on an airplane coming back from Jamaica with a broken heart, I built a brand-new house. In the beginning of my search, I would have been more than pleased to find an older house to buy. Actually, that was what I was looking for. I never thought that we could have afforded to build a new house, so I didn't even look at any. New houses are expensive, and we didn't have a lot of money to work with in the first place. Whoever would have thought that God had a brand-new house in mind for us? God certainly has a sense of humor!

Delayed Dreams

My daughter Shea-Marie has had her share of disappointments with God in the short twenty-three years that she has been on the planet. As I had mentioned before in the previous chapter, my daughter has always dreamed of becoming a dental hygienist from since she was a child, but to this day, she still hasn't accomplished her dream—yet! After she graduated from high school, she applied to the dental hygiene program at five different colleges. Since her grades had always been outstanding in high school, we just assumed that it wouldn't be a problem for her to get into college.

Her first choice was Fanshawe College, in London, Ontario, which is about seventy kilometers west of the small city that we lived in. The city of London wasn't as big as some of the other cities that she had applied to. That was a big part as to why Fanshawe College was her first choice. In a smaller city, she felt that it would be a safer environment for a young woman to live and attend school. As parents to one girl, we were a lot more protective of her and wanted to ensure her safety. So we were pleased with her choices, but we were hoping and praying that God would direct her footsteps to Fanshawe College.

She never got into any of them. She was placed on a waiting list at all five of the colleges that she had applied. She was distraught. That first year after high school, my husband got her a job at the courier company where he worked at. She worked there for a year and reapplied to the same five colleges the following year. Again, she never got into the dental hygiene program, but she got into the pre-health and science program. We encouraged her to accept the program at Fanshawe College, and she did.

She moved away from home to go to the college that she had dreamed about attending, but she was enrolled in a program that she didn't want to be in. Her thinking was that, at least, she got a foot through the doors, so next year, she would more likely get accepted to the dental hygiene program since she was already a student there. The next year, she applied again, and she wasn't accepted again! By this time, she was totally beside herself with grief, but she never gave up. She decided to enroll in the dental assistant program at the same college, and she got in. Both of these programs are a one-year program, and she graduated at the top of her class in both of them. One year, she even made the dean's list and had received a $3,000 bursary, but the next year, when she applied again for the fourth time, she wasn't accepted. She reluctantly decided to take her diploma in the dental assistant program and just stopped there.

Presently, she is working as a dental assistant, but she still hasn't given up on her dream. Her plan is to keep applying every year until she gets in. In the mean time, she's working and saving her money for when God finally opens the door. Every time my daughter didn't get into the hygiene program, we were all disappointed. We just couldn't understand why God kept closing the doors on her dream. I must have prayed a million prayers on her behalf, but it felt like the heavens were made of brass, and none of my prayers were getting through. I'm sure that at one time or another, we have all felt that way—like God had turned a deaf ear to our cries. Why hasn't God answer her prayers yet? That's simple—I don't know!

The Snowstorm

My brother Anthony told me an interesting story about a time in his life when he felt like God had disappointed him tremendously. One evening, he was driving home from work during a bad snowstorm. The roads were covered with ice. Almost like driving on an ice-skating rink. There were accidents everywhere. Cars had skidded of the roads and into ditches while others were just stranded on the side of the road. During the drive home, all Anthony could think about was getting home safely. All of a sudden, he noticed a car that had skidded off the road and was stuck in a snow bank. The driver was desperately trying to free it but was unsuccessful. Anthony, being the Good Samaritan that he is, stopped to help. The driver was a man, and he was very appreciative. It seems that he had been on the side of the road for some time and nobody had stopped to help him. After Anthony helped him and they both went their separate ways, Anthony lost control of his vehicle and kidded off the road.

He told me how long he was stranded on the side of the road trying hopelessly to dig his car out. He had found himself in the same predicament like the stranger he had just stopped to help, but nobody came to his rescue. Everybody drove past him, and there were no Good Samaritans. As he struggled to free himself, he thought of the irony of his situation and questioned God, in his heart, as to why He never provided a Good Samaritan to help him. To this day, he still wrestles with the disappointment of how God used him to help a stranger but never used anyone to help him. When I ask him how he got his car back on the road, he said, "I did it myself." Did God meet Anthony's need that day? Only Anthony can truly answer that question.

That is something I have always battled with for most of my life. Just like Anthony, I have always found myself in various predicaments where God would use me as a Good Samaritan, but whenever I was in trouble, it was only God who helped me. It would have been so easy to misconstrue God's love for me during those difficult times, and to be perfectly honest with you, I have—on many occasions. But it never lingers. I don't allow it to linger because I make it a point to remember the goodness of God. Whenever I am faced with a crisis, I draw from my memory bank all the times God came to our rescue. It's so easy for us to forget, especially when our life feels like a constant roller coaster.

Another Disappointment

Today, as I was writing the ending of this chapter, I received some disappointing news in the mail—again. It was a notification letter from the Ministry of Transportation about my driver's license. My license was suspended after I had suffered a brain injury in 2009. My neurosurgeon told me that he had to report my condition to the Ministry of Transportation—it's the law. But when I hadn't received anything from them notifying me that my license was suspended, I thought that maybe my doctor was wrong, but he wasn't. I was sitting at the computer when my husband handed me the letter. After I read it, I felt like someone had just punched me in the gut and knocked the wind out of me. It was my fault! It's not like my doctor hadn't warned me. Choosing to ignore it was ignorant. So there I was finishing up a chapter on disappointments when I had just experienced another disappointment.

Lately, it seems like my life has been one disappointment after another—with no end in sight. I keep getting these disappointing letters filled with bad news. Most of these letters, I have kept with the intentions of appealing them. But as much as I felt like I had just lost my independence even more than I already had, I still believe that every disappointment is for a reason. I may not understand what God is doing, but I still trust Him to do right by me. Sometimes I may feel like God has forsaken me like an orphan in a storm. And there are times when I am grasping to find the right words to say to Him to get Him to answer my prayers.

But if I get to the end of my life one day and find out that there is no God and that my entire existence has been a lie, it would only be another disappointment. Until then, I choose to believe that the God I serve is not made of wood or stone with the body of a man and the head of an animal. I choose to believe that I serve a living God who created me in His own image and likeness. Yes, disappointments hurt! And sometimes, they break you. But I refuse to live out the remainder of my days looking backward and wallowing in what might have been rather than moving forward and keep looking for those open doors. If the writing of this book turns out to be the greatest disappointment of my entire life, by sitting on a shelf somewhere gathering dust, then so be it. At least, I had a dream, and I had the guts to do something about it.

Behind the Scenes

Can we really know for sure what is good or bad? For instance, the airplane breaks down on the runway just before you, your entire family, and friends are to take a cruise to renew your vows on your twenty-fifth wedding anniversary. Or you suffer a ruptured brain aneurysm less than two months before you are to take your dream vacation to Australia for your fiftieth birthday. Or your daughter applying to the dental hygiene program four times and didn't get accepted. What about the disability claim that was denied? Sometimes it's hard to see how God is working behind the scenes.

Unfortunately, He doesn't usually show us where He's leading us or what He's doing and that can be very frustrating. Sometimes God's plans for us and our dreams don't always line up and we are often redirected by uncontrollable detours. God will reveal to us only what He chooses—nothing more. It's like driving a car at night, in a fog. Our headlights can only provide a limited amount of light for up to a limited amount of distant. But that doesn't stop us from getting to our destination. What prevents us from moving forward is only if we choose to turn back. We may find ourselves relying more heavily on our headlights when we are driving in poor weather conditions rather than under normal circumstances, but all we need is just enough light to keep us moving forward.

So it is with God. Perhaps He is leading us some place that we have never been before and the path that we're on is like driving in a fog or a blizzard. To make sure that we don't miss what God has planned for us, we must keep moving forward without straying from God's path. And if we know that God is the one who is leading us, we can trust His navigational skills to get us to our destination safely. This reminds me of a story that happened to my daughter and I a couple of years ago.

Out of the Blue

One Friday night, my daughter and I were driving back from the hairdresser which is about ninety kilometers east of the city where I live.

Earlier that morning when we left home, the sky was clear and the weather report didn't mention a single word about rain. It was a beautiful sunny day. After spending most the day at the hairdresser and we were anxious to beat the rush hour traffic going westbound to Kitchener where we live. We got off to a good start. The traffic was moving at a fairly normal pace, and if everything had gone well, we would have been home in about an hour.

But, out of the blue, it started raining. At first, it wasn't heavy—fairly light and sporadic. We had the radio on in our car listening to music, while we talked about our hair. We couldn't decide whether or not we were happy with the hairstyle that we had chosen. Being the cautious driver that I am, I wasn't in a hurry to get home. I normally drive in the middle or the slow lane—very seldom in the fast lane. My motto is to arrive alive. All of a sudden, we realized that the rain was falling more intensely in the west and we were heading right into it.

Everyone started to reduce their speed because our windshield wipers weren't moving fast enough to keep up with sudden downpour of heavy rain. I moved over into the far right lane, which is the slow lane, and reduce my speed almost down to a crawl. The visibility was extremely poor and we were in the middle of a thin fog. My daughter and I were beginning to get frightened because we couldn't see more than just a few feet ahead. We turned off the radio in the car to silence any distractions. At that moment any distractions, no matter how small, were not welcomed. Cars were pulling over on the side of the road for whatever reasons, but I wasn't about to pull over because I wanted to get home. I wanted to get out of that crazy weather even if I had to reduce my speed to 10 MPH.

I knew that even though I couldn't even see the tip of my nose in that fog, I wasn't going to stop. I was determined to get home. We prayed and ask God to release His angels around our vehicle and we kept on moving. Three hours later, my husband and children were relieved when they saw us pulled into our driveway safely. My daughter and I still talk about that dreaded night even to this day. The kind of fear that gripped our hearts that night was indescribable. And that is how I feel at times when God is taking me into parts unknown.

That's how I feel about moving back to Jamaica to retire after all these years. Don't get me wrong. I love Jamaica. I love the hot weather, wholesome foods and the beaches, but the crime rate is extremely high and that scares me. If it weren't for the fact that I believe that God is taking us back there for a greater purpose, I wouldn't even entertain the thought of ever going back. But I am still waiting for God to show me what He is doing behind the scenes before I uproot my family. I wish that I have the unshakeable faith that Abraham had, but I don't! Who knows! Maybe one day.

CHAPTER 6

Does God Always Meet Our Needs?

> And my God shall supply all your need according to His riches in glory by Christ Jesus.
>
> —Phil 4:19

The Letter

Today, only three days into a brand-new year, I was talking to my niece about some disappointing news that I had received earlier that day. I was extremely disappointed about a letter that I had received in the mail and was telling her how confident I was that God was going to work things out in my favor. But He didn't! After I read the letter, I ripped it into pieces, went into my bedroom, and wept! I needed a financial miracle and thought that God was going to work it out a certain way, but He didn't. I had been praying for years to come out of debt, but the more I prayed, the deeper we were spiraling into financial bankruptcy. Only the night before I received the letter, I was talking to my husband about it and was reassuring him that this could be God's way of getting us out of debt. I saw the way he looked at me. I could almost read his thoughts through his eyes. His eyes said, "There she goes again, always dreaming." He sees me as a dreamer and a prayer fanatic. I pray about everything, and I trust God implicitly. But sometimes, I think that I go overboard with my faith, and it makes me look like a fool when things don't work out the way I thought they would.

I was certain that God was going to get us out of debt with a disability claim that I was pursuing. But when the claim was denied, I felt like God had failed to meet my needs as He had promised. This time, I didn't look like a fool; I felt like one—a big one—and I was embarrassed. I believe that God is not a man that He should lie. And if the Bible says that we shouldn't be anxious for nothing, then I expect God to meet my needs. But you and I know that it's not that simple. Let's be honest. Has God always met your needs? I know what it's like to go to the grocery store with barely enough money to feed my family and have to ask the cashier to tell me when I'm getting close to the cutoff point. And when I can't afford to pay for all the groceries in my cart, I have to put the rest back in a long line of strangers glaring at me. Do you have any idea how humiliating that can be?

Yet we are told that as God's children, we are not to be anxious for nothing. Recently, during one of my sessions, I was talking to my therapist about the grocery store situation and how ashamed I was. He asked me if I felt like God had met my needs or He had failed to meet my expectations. He told me a story about a time in his life when he couldn't afford to pay his rent. He said that he had been praying to God to provide the money, but the money never came in. And to add insult to injury, God told him to go and asked the landlord for an extension. Then he repeated the question that he had asked me before. He said, "Do you think that God met your needs or did He fail to meet your expectations?"

I paused for a while. I thought about it carefully and said, "I think that God failed to meet both of our needs." He responded, "I disagree. God promises to meet our needs—not our expectations." He explained how he had felt the same way I did at first. But after God opened his eyes to the truth, he realized that his way of thinking was wrong. We both expected God to meet our needs in a certain way, and when He didn't, we thought that He had failed us. Whether God chose to grant the extension with the landlord or He allowed me to go through an embarrassing situation in the grocery store—either way, He provided.

God is not obligated to meet our expectations. He is obligated to meet our needs or else He is a liar! How He chooses to meet our needs doesn't always line up with our expectations, and when it doesn't, we feel like God has failed us. I'm sure that some may disagree with my interpretation of God's provision, and that's OK. I am not saying, by any means, that many don't go to bed at nights hungry and homeless. Jesus said in Matthew 26:11, "For you have the poor with you always." I believe that as long as the earth remains, there are always going to be sufferings and calamities. But in all my entire life, God has not once failed to meet my needs. I have not always received all that I have asked for—none of us has! Not even Jesus.

Remember when Jesus was about to die and He said, "O My Father, if it is possible, let this cup pass from me; nevertheless, not as I will, but as You will" (Matt. 26:39). What do you think Jesus was asking His Father? Jesus was praying to His Father and asking Him that if there was another way to accomplish His will except for Him to be crucified, then do it! There was no other way. So the answer was no. There's a huge difference between when God says *no* than when He has failed to meet our needs. I have shared some personal stories of the various ways God can meet our needs, and quite often, it's not what we think.

The Mechanic and the Man

This gentleman that I know shared a very touching story about the day his car broke down in another city. Frantically trying to find a mechanic, with only one hundred dollars in his wallet, he just happens to find a garage where he got his car fixed for eighty-five dollars. The man was furious that he had to spend most of his money to repair his car, leaving him with only fifteen dollars to get back home. During a conversation with the mechanic, he learned that the mechanic's business wasn't doing well to the point that he didn't even have money to buy food that day. The mechanic told the man that if he hadn't come into his shop that afternoon, he would have gone without food for the entire day. Do you still believe that God doesn't always meet our needs?

The beauty of the story is that God brought the mechanic and the man together so that they could meet each other's need. It wasn't a coincidence that the very day the mechanic needed money to buy food turned out to be the same day the man's car broke down in that city. And of all the garages for him to walk in, he walked into that one. The Bible says in Philippians 4:6, "Be anxious for nothing, but in everything by prayer and supplication, with thanksgiving, let your requests be made known to God." No matter what you are in need of today, God wants to meet those needs. Even if He has to break down somebody's car to pay your bills, He will do it. People, God works in mysterious ways, with wonders to perform. Don't make the same mistakes I used to make by trying to figure out what God is doing. You can't second-guess Him, even if you live to be a hundred years old. He's too big and too complicated for our tiny finite, human minds to unravel. Just ask Him for whatever you are in need of and trust Him to bring it to pass—His way!

The Car Accident

In 1986, when I was pregnant with my first child, Shea-Marie, my husband, Raffleton, was in a serious car accident. He was on his way home from work one evening when this elderly woman ran the red light and smashed into my husband's car. At that speed, it was a miracle that they both hadn't died, but both vehicles were completely destroyed. The insurance company paid us $5,000 for our car, and that was all the money we had to purchase another car. For weeks, my husband took the bus back and forth to work while we searched for another vehicle under $5,000.

I was pregnant and wasn't working at the time, so we were living on one income. And with the baby coming in a couple of months, money was tight, and we didn't want the added burden of another car loan. One day, my husband told me that he had a friend that was a mechanic, and he had asked this friend to help him find a good reliable car for under $5,000. Finally, the mechanic found a Volvo, which was my husband's favorite car in those days, and it was under $5,000. He asked for a $3,000 deposit up front to secure the vehicle and made arrangements with my husband for the balance upon delivery within a couple of days. That was the last time we saw or heard from the mechanic. He mysteriously disappeared with our $3,000, and we still didn't have a car.

We reported it the police and they tried to find him, but he was long gone, and so was our money. I can still remember the look on my husband's face when he realized that his own friend scammed him out of $3,000. That look is indelibly etched in my mind. We had to start the search all over again, but fortunately, we still had $2,000 left. We did what we should have done in the first place. We went to a reputable car dealership, used the $2,000 as a down payment, and bought a car. Yes, we had to finance the balance, and that's what we were trying to avoid in the first place. But in the end, God made it possible and provided a car for us even though it wasn't how we had planned it.

The Mexico Mission Trip

In 1995, after my uncle committed suicide and I had suffered yet the loss of another child, I was asked by my pastor, along with eight other people, to go to Mexico with the church. Our church had been doing missionary work in Mexico with the children on the dumps for many years.

The cost of the trip was $1,500, and I didn't have it. I had just recently had a miscarriage and was in pretty bad shape emotionally. The only reason why I was even contemplating taking the trip was to take my mind off of what I had lost. In a way, the trip was a blessing in disguise.

I figured that if God really wanted me to go, He would provide the money that I needed before the deadline. Out of the blue, a check showed up in the mail for $1,503. I knew right away that God had provided the money for the trip, but my husband thought otherwise. My husband was not a spiritual man at all. We never saw eye to eye on anything remotely related to God. I was more of a dreamer who married a realist, which makes strange bedfellows. My husband believed that if you want something, you get it the good old-fashioned way—work for it! I, on the other hand, pray about everything.

If we didn't have it, I'd pray for it, and I expected to get it. It's that's simple! As far as I was concerned, the money was mine. But my husband didn't see it that way. He saw the bills, and that was final. He agreed to give me half of the money, and at least, half was better than nothing. I had $750, and time was running out! I cleaned houses, sold chocolate bars door-to-door, held garage sales—whatever it took; I did it to raise the money. At the eleventh hour, just before the deadline, I raised $1,500 to pay for my trip—again! I was disappointed with my husband for a very long time because I believed that the money was an answer to my prayers for the trip, and the very thing that my husband criticized me for—being a prayer fanatic—worked! Sometimes, like with the foreclosure of my house, God doesn't always work things out quite the way we anticipate, but He chooses to do it; I have learned to accept that God always knows what's best for His children.

The Eleventh Hour

During the course of my life, I have seen God do the strangest things, things that I would have never imagined in a thousand years. On September 30, 2010, God did something remarkable for our family. My son Jordan had just returned to college after he dropped out the year before. He came home from school for the Christmas holidays and announced to everyone that he wasn't returning. As much as his father and I pleaded with him about throwing away his education, he wouldn't listen! He was obdurate! At that time, I had just recently been released from the hospital from having brain surgery, so my condition was precarious. I knew that arguing with him would worsen my condition and possibly put me back into the hospital. So my husband and I decided to turn it over to God and let Him handle it.

A few weeks later, early in the morning, after being up all night agonizing over what to say to my son to get him to go back to school, I started praying, and I heard this still, small voice impressed upon my heart to leave my son alone; I just about fell out of bed when I heard it. This was the second time I had heard the same thing regarding this same child. The first time was about two years prior when my son had just graduated from high school and was trying to decide which college he wanted to attend. He had received a scholarship from a school in the United States, and although he was pleased about it, he wasn't thrilled! This school was a division three (D3) college, and in the world of sports, mainly basketball, that is considered to be the lowest level.

From my son was old enough to hold a basketball, he had always dreamed of playing professional basketball. And he was a pretty good baller too. I named him Jordan, not after his idol, Michael Jordan. That was purely coincidental. As Christian parents, I had hoped that my son would become an evangelist, like Billy Graham, or at least, a pastor. But he wanted to play basketball for a living. That's why we were shocked when he turned down the basketball scholarship. Come to find out that he was holding out for a better offer, which never came. We were all disappointed. I urged my son on several occasions to accept the offer, but once again, he was obstinate. That's when I heard the voice of God telling me for the first time to leave him alone. After the Christmas holidays were over and the kids were going back to school, my son was looking for a job with only a high school diploma under his belt. I wasn't jumping up and down when he went back to work for a company that he had worked for during the summer. I didn't want to see him throw his future away working twelve-hour shifts, assembling BlackBerry cell phones, but God had a sense of humor. It just about drove me crazy keeping my mouth shut as I watched him drag himself out of bed in the wee hours of the mornings or late at nights, working a mediocre job, when I knew in my heart that God had so much more for him. But God told me to zip my lips, and I zipped it!

By the time summer rolled around, he was anxious to go back to school. We couldn't have been more pleased to watch him choose his program, apply for a student loan, and look for an apartment all on his own. We were proud parents when the first week of September came and he was heading back to college. It almost felt like the first day we took him to preschool when he was only four years old. At least then, he was only in school half days, and by the time I walked back home, I would have to turn around and go back to pick him up.

This time it was different. We were loading up a truck packed with everything that he owned and moving our baby boy into his own place, ninety kilometers away from home for the next two years, again! Remember, we did this the year before? This was the second time, and it hurt just as much as it did the first time—maybe worse! I did everything in my power to stop the tears from flowing. I hugged him and told him how proud I was of him and that he had made the right decision to return to school. Then only a month later, when the second rent payment on my son's apartment was due, my son's student loan hadn't come in, and we didn't have any money. We needed to come up with $1,000 in twenty-four hours, and we had no idea how we were going to cover the rent.

My husband and I didn't sleep a wink the night before. We spent the entire night tossing and turning, trying to figure out how we were going to come up with the money. The next morning, my eyes were swollen and bloodshot red from crying and praying. I prayed earnestly for God to meet our needs and to provide the money that we needed. As I was praying, I thought to myself, "This must be how Jesus felt in the garden of Gethsemane when he prayed until his sweat became drops of blood." As I knelt beside my bed crying, I clearly remember this overwhelming sense of peace that enveloped me as if to let me know that everything was going to be all right.

So I got up, went into the bathroom, washed my face, and went about my day. As the hours passed by and midday rolled around, I saw God supernaturally brought in the money before the end of the day. I remember asking God to work a miracle on my behalf and show my husband and children how great He is. I wanted to encourage my family to believe God to do the impossible in their lives. If I could accomplish that, then I know that my children would go on to do great things in their lives. You should have seen the look on their faces—they were dumbfounded! God brought the money in at the eleventh hour, but unfortunately, my son's student loan still hadn't come in yet!

The Confirmation

Three weeks had gone by since God gave us the money to pay our son's rent in college, but that was just one need. My son needed books, school supplies, and much more . . . but still, the student loan money hadn't come in. It was already six weeks into the school term, and my son had no books. It was hard on him and us too. I had been praying all along, every day to be exact. Even though the money was being held back for some reason, we knew that we hadn't made a mistake in sending him back to college. And if we were certain that we had the mind of God concerning our son's future, then God had to release the funds sooner or later. More than anything else, more than how much we needed God to release the money, we needed to know that we could trust Him in everything. Then on top of everything else, our own house payment was due in a couple of days, and we didn't have that either! I had seen God come through for us more times than some people have ever seen in their lifetime. I trusted Him. I had proven Him. And I needed to prove him again! I had to know wherever God was leading us, He would take care of us and that was important to me.

We were all too familiar with the predicament we had found ourselves in. After twenty-seven years of marriage, we had been there countless times. I kept reassuring my husband and myself of the faithfulness of God and that God had never abandoned us before. But after several weeks of praying into the wee hours of the morning, nothing happened! Then the time came for us to make one of the most painful decisions of our lives or just sit back and watch everything that we worked so hard for fall apart. It was early one Saturday morning, three days before the deadline. My husband had gone in to work from the night before, and I was lying in bed praying.

I hadn't slept too well the night before because I was a bit apprehensive about talking to my husband about the possibility of us taking our son out of school. I felt confused as to why God hadn't answered our prayers, and the decision that we had to make was gut wrenching. I wanted to pray again and again, but my heart felt too heavy. Furthermore, I didn't know the magic words that would miraculously move the hand of God in our favor. I got out of bed, made myself a cup of herbal tea, and sat down in the living room, staring out the big bay window. I wondered, "How are we going to tell Jordan that we have to take him out of school." My mind was exhausted from trying to figure out what I was going to say to my husband when he came home.

"God, where are you?" I cried! I had been praying vigilantly without an answer. I was really starting to have doubts. My faith was waning with each passing hour. I kept saying over and over, "God, where are you, God, where are you." I wasn't about to cave in now. As the day progressed, all I could think about were the million of times God had provided for us over the years. I couldn't give up my faith now, not after all these years. What would I have left? "God, I made a promise to you that I wouldn't go back to that dark place," I said. All day long, this song kept playing repeatedly in my head. "He'll do it again." Everything was riding on what God was going to do in this situation.

What about all the dreams I thought God had given me for my life. Will I ever be certain that it was God? And if I couldn't trust God to meet my needs, then all would be lost. That Saturday night, before I went to bed, I told God I wasn't going to pray anymore. I knew in my heart that I had done everything humanly possible, and the rest was up to Him. The next morning, Sunday morning, I decided to go to church, which I hadn't done in a long time. By the time church was over and I got home, my son had called to tell us that his student loan money was in his bank account. It had been sitting there for two days without his knowledge.

God had already answered our prayers, and we didn't know it. God had already proven to us that we could trust Him to provide for us like a father provides for his children. We were able to pay our mortgage, purchase books and school supplies for our son, and made a decision not to pull our son out of college. In a nutshell, God had told me about a year before this to start making preparations for our retirement. That involved moving back to Jamaica away from my extended family. I had questioned God about what I thought I had heard and had asked Him to use this situation to confirm it. I couldn't just pack up our belongings and move thousands of miles away to a country that I hadn't called home for almost forty years. I was terrified! What if God didn't tell me to return to my homeland? How would we provide for ourselves once we got there? But after the money came in the way it did, I knew in my heart what I had to do. The only way to know if God is speaking to you is to do the last thing you think He told you to do.

Unshakeable Faith!

Before then, I often wondered how Abraham must have felt when God told him to leave his country, his family, and his father's house. To go somewhere God hadn't even told him yet (Gen. 12:1). Can you imagine selling your house, taking your kids out of school, uprooting them from their family and friends, and starting driving to parts unknown? I don't know if I would be brave enough. Furthermore, my children would have led a mutiny against us. But Abraham did it, and he never said a word. He never questioned God. He just loaded down his camels, gathered his wives and children, and ventured out into the middle of nowhere. Now, that's what you call unshakeable faith!

Henry Blackaby, author of *Created to be God's Friend*, said, "To know the ways of God clearly is to know how to recognize when He is working in and around your own life. This alerts you to respond—knowingly. You will know what awaits you (1) if you respond by yielding your life unconditionally to Him; and (2) you will know clearly what you will forfeit, or miss, if you say, 'No!' to God." I wish that I could be more like Abraham when it comes to doing the will of God. At least, I know where God is leading me—Abraham didn't! And yet, I still find it hard to take that giant leap of faith.

Let's face it. I'm not alone. Most of us find it difficult, if not impossible, to distinguish God's voice from all the others voices that we hear; even when we're almost certain that God told us to do something, we still find excuses not to do it. How many answers to prayers have we missed because of fear? Unshakeable faith, like Abraham's, is a gift from God. It's called the gift of faith. The gift of faith is one of the nine gifts of the Holy Spirit found in First Corinthians 12:9. When someone is operating in the gift of faith, like Abraham, that person will believe God no matter what. God told Abraham when he was a hundred years old and his wife, Sarah, was ninety that they were going to have a son (Gen. 17). Would you have believed? I wouldn't!

Enter His Rest

On October 11, 2009, I suffered a ruptured brain aneurysm and was in a coma. (I will tell you all about it in chapter 8.) While I was in a coma, God did something remarkable in our finance. In our household, I take care of the finance, which includes paying all the bills. My husband had always entrusted me to pay the bills, so when I was hospitalized, he was like a fish out of water. He didn't have a clue what bills were due on what date and the payment method I was using. At that time, we also had two children in college and with tuition payments and rent payments on their apartment; we were up to our eyeballs in debt. The bills were piling up, and we didn't have any money in the bank to pay them. Since I was the one who knew how to stretch a buck into two, my husband felt lost. With me being so sick and all, he desperately wanted to take some time off from work to focus on me and the children, but he couldn't afford to. Feeling completely inundated by my illness and trying to be there for the children and paying the bills, he had nowhere else to turn but to God.

One afternoon, he went into the bank to pay some bills, and when he looked inside the bank book after the teller gave it back to him, he almost had a heart attack. There was a mysterious deposit for $5,000. My husband ran out of the bank faster than Usain Bolt, the fastest man in the world. After I came out of the coma, he couldn't wait to tell me what had happened and showed me the passbook as proof. Neither one of us had a clue where all that money came from until sometime later when we traced it. It was a tax amendment refund that we had filed over six months prior. We had completely forgotten all about it because we weren't sure if we were even qualified to receive the adjustment.

The Bible says, "Look at the birds of the air, for they neither sow nor reap nor gather into barns; yet your Heavenly Father feeds them. Are you not of more value than they?" (Matt. 6:26). God knows what we need, and He promises to meet our needs—not our expectations. Do you think that the mysterious deposit in our bank account was just a coincidence? Of course not! Of all the times for it to show up was when we needed it the most. Recently, I saw a picture hanging on a wall in an office that moved me. It was a picture of a lighthouse in the middle of the ocean during a storm. Below the lighthouse, the water was fiercely raging, splashing rigorously against the base of the lighthouse. In one of the doorways, leaning peacefully against the doorframe was a man with both hands in his pockets.

The picture painted a thousand words of someone who appeared to be stress free. The man was just chilling! The picture inspired me. I stared at the man in the picture wishing it was me. I envied him for the peace that I saw on his face. The way his body language spoke in volumes of the stillness in his soul. Oh, how I longed to get to a place in Christ where I could just chill out with my hands in my pockets in the midst of a crisis, knowing that God was in control of my storms. Being confident that God was my lighthouse and He was going to fix everything that was broken in my life and in my body as He had promised in His word. Oh how I longed to enter into His rest with the assurance that God is my provider and my constant friend.

I caught a glimpse of the kind of life God wants us to live, in that picture, and my life hasn't been the same since. All these years worrying about everything and accomplishing nothing was just a waste. Psalms 37:8 says, "Do not fret—it only causes harm." Harm to our health, harm in our relationships and to our peace of mind. Worrying about our problems isn't worth getting sick over. Remember the children of Israel in the Bible? The Bible said that God provided for all of them for forty years in the wilderness. Even their clothes and shoes didn't wear out in forty years, and they didn't go out of style either.

Be Anxious for Nothing

I don't know about you, but sometimes I feel like God is just chilling out in heaven, with His hands in His pockets, just watching, while my life is falling apart at the seams. I feel like He's not doing anything, neither does He intend to because my situation hasn't change one bit. I have news for you. God isn't anxious about anything. He's in total control of everything. Not because we're freaking out, ringing our hands, trying to figure out how in the world we're going to get out of the mess that we're in, means that God doesn't care about us. That's why He told us not to be anxious for nothing. Nothing means everything—our finance, our health, our children. Everything! God hasn't abandoned us, no matter what it looks like.

It has been said that when God seems the most absent, He is the most present. He is in the middle of our circumstances, whether or not we have recognized Him. In Chapter two, I talked briefly about God performing a miracle on my brother Mario's eye in 1997. When Mario was four years old, one of our brothers threw a piece of broken glass and hit him in the left eye, which left him totally blind in that eye for more than twenty years. In 1997, he picked up an infection in his right eye and it was surgically removed.

Miraculously, God restored sight to his left eye immediately after his right eye was removed. With the help of prescription glasses and regular check ups with his Ophthalmologist, he has been able to live a fairly normal life for the past fourteen years. Until recently, in 2011, he picked up an infection in the same eye, but I wasn't aware of it. For several days, my brother had been heavily on my mind. I just had a strange feeling that something was wrong with him but I didn't do anything about it for days. Because I had been going through my own difficulties in my health, I kept ignoring the impressions in my heart about my brother. Call it a woman's intuition or whatever; I just knew that something bad was happening to my brother.

After a while, I just couldn't stand it anymore, I had to call to see what was wrong. It was then that I learned that he had picked up an infection in his eye and he needed to have surgery in order to save the eye, but he couldn't afford it. Up to that point, he was anxious about how he was going to raise the money for the surgery. I just happened to call at the right time. It was a lot of money and I didn't have that much money to help him. I told him that I would call him back, and I hung up the telephone. I immediately prayed and asked God to tell me what to do. I felt that God wanted me to call my pastor to see if the church would do something to help me raise the money.

My pastor said that he would help, but he encouraged me to seek out others for donations. I started calling the people that I felt that God had laid on my heart to ask. One by one, they all said that they would help. Some giving as little as $20 up to $100. Within three weeks, I raised more than what I needed to pay for the surgery. God used the most unlikely people—people that didn't even know my brother personally to give money to save his eye. It didn't matter that times were tough and a lot of people were out of work. Everyone that I called made a commitment to give something. In the end, God provided for my brother again. It was amazing!

A Fear of Dying

I am fifty-one years old, and I know in my heart of hearts that I am not going to die not even one day before my ninetieth birthday. I have always said it, and I firmly believe it. I heard a story about a man who was still practicing law at 101 years old. This attorney would be up every morning by 5 am, ate a hearty breakfast, and was at his law office by 6:30 a.m. ready to begin his day. When asked the secret of his long life, he smiled and said, "Not dying." For many years, I used to worry about dying. My biggest fear was dying a slow and painful death, like my mother-in-law. She died of ovarian cancer in 1998. Actually, that's when this fear of dying all started. One day, I remembered asking God to take away the fear because it was starting to paralyze me. Every time I thought about dying, which was often, I would get these panic attacks. I knew that it wasn't the will of God for me to live my life in a constant state of fear. I had no idea how God was going to deliver me from the fear of dying, but I was confident that He would. When the Bible said that we are not to be anxious for nothing—that even means the fear of death. So when I prayed and ask God to deliver me from this awful fear, He answered my prayer.

On October 11, 2009, when I suffered the brain aneurysm, that was when God delivered me. God used a near-death experience to take away my fear of death—that was brilliant! It was then I realized that death is not this horrible, dark, painful journey that one takes alone. It's a journey that God takes with you. It's a personal thing between you and a loving God. After I came out of the coma, I had no recollection of what had happened—even to this day! It was then I realized that if I had died on that day, it would have been a quick and painless death—just like I had prayed for after I witnessed my mother-in-law's death. I actually prayed and asked God that when my time comes, I wanted to die a quick death, and I almost did. Some time during my coma, something must have happened because when I woke up, I was not afraid of dying anymore. God cares about everything that we care about—no matter what that is.

Embarrassing Stuff

Whether our need is financial, sickness, fear, rejection . . . God promises to meet them, and He will. Like the lawyer who was still practicing law at 101 years old, he attributed his long life and success to seeing the hand of God upon his life—his whole life. I am going to share some embarrassing stuff that has happened to me during the course of my life, but in all of them, I have seen the hand of God's provisions and protection upon my life—my whole life. This particular story really pains me every time I think about it, but I have chosen to share it with you just in case there are others out there that can empathize with it. In the previous chapter, chapter 5, on disappointments, I talked about my first wedding ceremony on December 3, 1983, when my husband gave me a $50 engagement ring, vowing that one day he would replace it with a more deserving one. He kept his promise. On our twenty-fifth wedding anniversary in 2008, he replaced it with the most exquisite diamond ring. I cherish it! When my son was returning to college in the fall of 2010, we were experiencing some financial difficulties, and I had to pawn my most cherished possession to help pay for his tuition. As embarrassing as that was, I never flint. Even though I waited twenty-five years for my ring and I had it only two years before it ended up in the pawnshop, it was just a possession—something that was bought.

There's nothing in this world that is more important to me than my family. Parents do whatever it takes to provide for their children. The Bible said that if we, as earthly parents, who are limited, can give our children good gifts, God, who is sovereign, can do far more. If you ever find yourself pawning your most cherished possessions or having to do a payday loan or borrow money from a friend or relative to make ends meet—do it! There's no shame in it. In my opinion, the only thing we shouldn't do for our children is steal. No matter what! Beg, if you have to, but never steal. There are no justifications for that. So whether it's a trip to the pawnshop or the payday loan store, it's still God's provision. Actually, I must admit that I was one of those people that never thought about doing embarrassing things to pay my bills as God's provision. I thought that God had failed to meet my needs as He had promised. It wasn't until after my therapist had opened my eyes to all the various ways God uses to meet our needs on a daily basis before I accepted it.

The Record Collection

In 2007, when my daughter Shea-Marie was accepted into the pre-health and science program at Fanshawe College, although that wasn't the program she had applied to originally, we were proud parents. As we were preparing to find her an apartment, furnish it and pay the tuition fee, we didn't have a lot of money. My husband was a professional DJ when we first met and had a vast collection of records that he had accumulated over the years. They were his prized possession. One day, he came home and told me that he was going to sell them in order to help pay for our daughter's college tuition. I knew how much he loved the records, so I urged him to take some time to think it through thoroughly before making a decision. He was adamant that selling the records were the only recourse that was available to us and so I agreed. One evening, we stopped into one of our favorite restaurants to place an order for takeout.

While we were waiting for our food, my husband saw a table in a corner of the restaurant that had some flyers on it. He went over to it and started browsing through the flyers. He came across a flyer of a young man looking to buy old records—the kind of records that my husband had. My husband picked up the flyer and took it home, but he never made contact for some time. I think that as much as he really wanted to get the money to help pay for our daughter's education, those records were a significant part of his past. There were a lot of sentiments attached to them. When he finally made the decision to sell, he called and set up a meeting with the buyer on a day when he knew I had to go out. When I returned home, he had $5,000 in cash in an envelope.

He handed me the envelope, and I couldn't believe my eyes when I saw what was in it. He told me what he had done, and I really didn't know what to think about what he had done, especially since he hadn't spoken to me about it first. Although I was happy about the money, I was sad that he felt that he had to make such a sacrifice. I asked him how many records he had sold to get that much money, and he said, "All of them." I replied, "All of them? You didn't leave anything for us to dance to?" When I looked into the garage where he kept the records, all of them were gone, except for one: the one that we danced to at our wedding—"Misty" by Johnny Mathis. Apparently, the buyer wanted all of them, but my husband couldn't part with that one. I was touched by the sentiment he showed by not selling our song. We used the money to pay for my daughter's tuition for her first year of college. It was the most unselfish expression of a father's love that I had ever witnessed. That day, my husband became a hero—not only in my daughter's eyes, but also in mine. Did God meet our need that day? He most certainly did!

God Has the Final Word

As long as we are alive, we are going to have needs, but God doesn't want us to be overwhelmed by them; He wants us to trust Him to meet them one need at a time. After I had my first miscarriage at seventeen years old, the doctors told me that I may never have children. I could have allowed that devastating news to dictate my future, but I didn't. I never accepted it as being final. God hadn't spoken yet. And God's words are the only ones that truly matters. I knew the doctors were only speaking from a medical point of view. And in the natural scope of things, they were correct. But I wanted a baby, and I wasn't about to take no for an answer. I had a need, and God said that He would supply my need. So for three years, I fasted, prayed, and I refused to quit. And God remembered me and gave me three beautiful children.

CHAPTER 7

How To Forgive

The Unthinkable!

Love all, trust a few, do wrong to none.
—William Shakespeare

What Does It Mean to Forgive?

The word "forgive" means "to cease to feel resentment against an offender. Pardon one's enemies." When I read that for the first time, I said to myself, "That's impossible! I couldn't imagine not feeling any resentment at all, no matter how small, for someone that had deeply hurt me! As time passes, I may feel less resentment compared to when the offense initially happened, but to cease to feel any resentment at all is impossible." That's what I truly believed, until I learned about "the power of relinquishment." You can learn how to let go of resentments that you've been carrying for decades but only if you really want to. This is what I hope to accomplish in this chapter.

One of the greatest, heartfelt stories about true forgiveness I have ever heard was in an interview on a sport television program called *Homecoming*. Basketball legend Irvin Magic Johnson was being interviewed, and when asked about the day when he first learned that he had HIV, he said the most amazing thing. He said that when he went home and told his wife that he had tested positive for the HIV virus, he told her that if she wanted to leave the marriage, he would understand. At that time, his wife was pregnant. But instead of doing what most women would have done in her situation, which would be to leave the marriage, she hit him upside the head and asked him what was wrong with him. Then she suggested that they pray about it. I was moved to tears as my husband and I watched this couple more than nineteen years later, still very much in love with one another. This woman personifies the meaning of the word "forgiveness."

When Someone That You Trust Rejects You

Several years ago, one of my most dearest and trusted friend of twenty-five years ended our friendship without one word of an explanation. In the beginning, I grieved the loss of the friendship almost as if my friend had died. I was confused as to why I was taking it so hard. After all, it wasn't as if I had never lost a friendship before. My behavior was bizarre, and I didn't know why. I remember telling my sister Rose how surprised I was by the way I was dealing with it. The pain and deep sense of loss that I was experiencing didn't make any sense to me at all. I thought to myself, *What's wrong with you, Althea? It's not like your friend is dead you know.* In my opinion, the worst kind of pain that anyone could ever experience in their lifetime would be the death of a child, and that had already happened to me more times than I cared to remember.

I was all too familiar with the pain of losing a loved one to death. But my friend wasn't dead! This individual was very much alive! *So what was my problem?* I wondered. Later, I found out that what I was experiencing was grief, and anger and sadness are two of the most common aspects of grieving. For some strange reason unbeknown to me, I was grieving the loss of the friendship in the same way I would grieve the death of a loved one. There were times when my emotions felt raw and exposed. I was overly sensitive to everything, even to the slightest insignificant things. I would lose my temper at the drop of a hat, almost like someone kept flipping a switch on and off in my brain. One minute, I felt angry, cold as ice, mean like a junkyard dog. And the next minute, I would be sobbing uncontrollably.

This bizarre behavior went on for two years. Day after day, a little bit at a time, I would detach myself from reality and slowly withdrew into this emotional cocoon. I had built up walls around myself in hopes of keeping people out. I had to make sure that no one could ever get close enough to me to hurt me like that again. Subsequently, I went into denial, not knowing that grieving begins with denial (refusing to believe that my best friend had rejected me) and ends with acceptance (coming to terms with the reality that the friendship was lost.) One day, my sister Rose gave me a book called *When I Lay My Isaac Down* by Carol Kent. My sister thought that the book might help me to let go of the pain of rejection. She was absolutely right! God used the book to show me that it was perfectly normal to grieve the loss of the friendship.

The reality of the situation was I had suffered a loss—the loss of the friendship. And even though my mind was telling me that my friend was still alive and we can't grieve someone that is not dead, my heart was saying otherwise. Someone doesn't have to die in order for us to experience grief. Grief is a natural emotion that follows the absence of someone or something from our life. To a person that is incarcerated, he/she has lost their freedom. A miscarriage is the loss of a potential offspring. To the widow/widower, he/she has lost their life's partner and friend. Whether that someone leaves your life by the way of death, divorce, or they choose to walk away, like my friend, it's still a loss, and the loss must be grieved.

In my case, it wasn't only the loss of the friendship I was grieving. I was also experiencing shame, rejection, and worthlessness. Somehow I had lost my self-esteem and self-worth, but I didn't realize it until God used the book to unveil all the other emotions that were hidden beneath my pain. The pain of rejection and abandonment in my heart was poisonous. It was slowly poisoning my other relationships. I kept telling myself that I was a bad person or else my friend wouldn't have rejected me while all along, God was telling me how much I was loved by many others, especially Him. But the only voice I was fixed on was my own, telling me that nobody loved me, and it was only a matter of time before everyone, even God, would abandon me—like my friend had. I felt so unloved and unworthy to be loved, not just by the person that had rejected me, but by everyone, even God. I had allowed the rejection of one person to infiltrate my other relationships to the extent that I was starting to push away the people who truly loved and appreciated me.

I thought that if I rejected them first, it would save me the anguish of when they finally reject me. I was a mess! I was a train wreck waiting to happen. My heart wasn't big enough to hold the amount of pain and despair that I was experiencing. Carol Kent's book also talked about relinquishing our pain to God, and while I was reading it, I suddenly burst into tears. I must have cried for hours because when I finally stopped, I felt like my tears had washed away the poison that had infested my heart. And for the first time, I felt hopeful.

Power of Relinquishment

The word relinquishment means, "To yield, surrender, to give up completely." Carol Kent, author of *When I Lay My Isaac Down* said, "But when we release our grasp, our relinquishment puts a stop to our manipulation of other people and releases the Holy Spirit to do the supernatural through the power of prayer: It's an act of trusting God when we cannot envision a positive outcome." Wow! Those words leaped off the page of the book and aimed straight to my broken heart like Cupid's arrow. For me—the problem was, I was full of anger and resentment toward this person and I wanted revenge. I wanted to control the outcome of the object of my concern by manipulation God into avenging me the way I wanted Him to.

I didn't want to trust God to deal with my friend in His way. I was afraid that God would be too merciful. But when I relinquished my grasp, it became an act of faith in God to bring about a positive outcome. You see, God didn't just want to do a work in my friend's heart alone, he wanted to do a work in my heart, too. By the time I had finished reading the book, the attitude of my heart had changed. I made a decision to let God vindicate me in His way and in His time. Even though my flesh was kicking up a stink, I needed to prove God when the Bible tells us that vengeance belongs to God alone, and He will repay us. It was in that moment, I started my journey of forgiveness.

When you have truly forgiven someone, your feelings of resentment no longer exist. You may not trust them or even like them, but you no longer hold any ill will toward them. There may be times when something triggers the hurt and those old painful memories come flooding back like a tsunami. When that happens, it doesn't mean that you haven't forgiven the people that have hurt you. It just means that God is not finish yet! Forgiveness is a work in progress! In the beginning, after my friend rejected me, I couldn't hear this person's name without blowing a gasket. Even the thought of crossing path with that person would send me straight into orbit. But after I made the decision to forgive, I found myself more susceptible to the will of God. Choosing forgiveness is not an instant recipe for freedom. It's a day-to-day process, and it's slow. But if you stay the course—over time—it will work.

Forgiveness Is a Choice!

When someone we love hurts us and we think that we can never forgive them, we can! We can forgive the unthinkable! But we can't do it on our own strength no matter how hard we try. True forgiveness isn't about feelings. True forgiveness is a choice! It's a decision that we have to make to choose forgiveness over bitterness and then trust God to set things right. I remember how relieved I was the first time I heard that. I said, "No wonder why it wasn't working." I had been trying for years to forgive people that had hurt me, but in my heart, I was still angry. I didn't want to be around them in anyway, not even in church. But when I heard that forgiveness starts with making a decision to forgive, and eventually, our heart will catch up, I was relieved! It was finally starting to make sense now. After that, I would walk around, saying, "I forgive my friend. I forgive the man that molested me when I was a child. I forgive my father for walking out on my mother."

I kept saying it as often as I would remember, until one day, my heart caught up with my mouth. This transformation took place by faith—faith in what I was saying. And it didn't happen overnight—it took a very long time!

Forgiving the One You Love

When we are in the process of forgiving someone that we love, there's an internal conflict that takes place within our heart. We become torn, for there is another part of us that is petrified. As much as we know that we have already forgiven that person, there's a matter of trust that we need to resolve. We think that if we let those individuals back into our lives, we are afraid that we might be sending them the wrong message that they can do whatever they want to us and we will forgive them. Trust is something that takes time to establish, but it can be easily broken with just one act of betrayal. Recently, my daughter broke up with her boyfriend after they had been dating for four years. I watched her literally go through hell when her boyfriend asked her to take him back. She was still in love with him, but he had hurt her deeply, and she didn't trust him anymore. The trust had been breached. And as a result, her perception of him had changed. In fact, she was afraid of him, and that kind of fear, I was well acquainted with.

When my daughter asked me what she should do, I couldn't instruct her. Once someone has wronged you, it's done! You can't undo the wrong. And you can't just hand them your heart on a silver platter for them to break it again. It's not easy to get up, brush yourself off, and start all over again either. Trust has to be earned, and sometimes, it's impossible! I don't know what she intends to do, but I'm hoping that she won't take him back. I hope that she takes a step back and remember that God had already told her that this man wasn't right for her.

Forgiving the Dead

Recently, I went to the funeral service, to say farewell to a great man of God. He was ninety-one years old. He was the founding pastor of a thriving church, which he handed over the reigns to his only son, when he retired years ago. Four months before his death, the church celebrated fifty years in ministry. When this great man of God started out, he and his wife, and their two children, started out with a total of fifteen people in their home. One day, this pastor claimed that he had heard the audible voice of God telling him to go and start a church. His obedience kicked into gear, and proved to everyone that he had indeed heard the voice of God. For a country bumpkin born and raised on a farm, he touched the lives of countless people all over the world.

He pioneered many churches, built orphanages, schools, and Christian outreaches all over the world. In countries like Canada, United States, India, Jamaica, Mexico, Haiti, Africa and many more—touching the lives of thousands, including my family for many years. My husband and I were married in his church in 1983, and all three of our children were dedicated there as well. He survived his precious wife, who died many years before him. He poured his heart and soul into the church doing what he loved to do—serving God and serving others. The funeral service was held at his church, with hundreds in attendance. It was a sight to behold! I supposed he always knew that the church he built would one day house his remains on the day of his funeral, and I'm sure that's what he requested.

I arrived at the church about fifteen minutes before the service began, and it was almost standing room only. I managed to finagle a seat way up in the balcony. Even though everyone looked like dwarfs from up there, at least, I was sitting. One by one, the deceased grandchildren, his neighbor of forty-seven years, colleagues, board members and many others took the microphone and heaped a multitude of accolades upon the dearly departed. While I was sitting there listening to all the wonderful tributes to this man of God, it got me thinking about all the people in our lives that we wait until they are dead before we sing their praises in songs and recite poems and shed bitter tears. I don't want to be guilty of that. The dead can't hear anything, neither can they speak. I want to make sure that I say all the things that I need to say to the people that I love or to the ones that I have offended before death silence me. I want to be certain to right the wrongs that I may be guilty of and to give closure to someone that I have deeply wounded—whether knowingly or ignorantly before the curtain of my life falls and all opportunities are lost forever!

I know a woman who was deeply wounded by someone who never apologized to her before he died. She waited many years for this person to come and say those three little words, "I am sorry," but he never came. He went to his grave without giving her the closure that she needed and it was quite a blow when she realized that she was never going to hear those words. When she first learned of his death, she couldn't even put her emotions into words. She was dumbfounded! After all, it was over! The offender was dead but what about the offended? How do we forgive the dead and find closure? We do it in the same way we would, as if the person was still alive—by faith! And by trusting God that one day He will right the wrong that has been done to us.

It's senseless to keep harboring resentful feelings towards someone that is dead. There comes a time when we have to relinquish it to God. There is no repentance from the grave. Many of us are walking around infested with hate towards someone who is dead. What's done is done. It's time to release the deceased. Now, it's up to God to judge an unrepentant heart. The bible says that we have to work out our own salvation. I take that seriously. I don't want to live my entire life thinking that I'm going to make heaven when I die, only to wind up lost because of unforgiveness. It's just not worth losing heaven over. If you know in your heart that you have deeply hurt someone and you still haven't made it right, don't keep putting it off. Do the right thing and apologize to them before it's too late. Your eternity may very well depend upon it.

Revenge Is Not an Option

When we have been hurt, our flesh demands justice, and for most of us, that's revenge! It's quite natural for us to desire justice and to want to see the offender pay for his or her transgressions. But it's not up to us to take matters into our own hands. Revenge can never bring relief to our wounded soul! Seeking revenge (justice) is never the answer; it only compounds the situation and makes matters worse. Hurt people hurt people, and the cycle continues until all is lost! You see this kind of behavior when two people are going through a bitter divorce. Bitter, resentful people not only destroy themselves but also hurt those that are dearest to their hearts. Put down your weapon of war—revenge—and clothe yourself with love. It's your only option! Martin Luther King Jr. said, "Man must evolve for all human conflict a method which rejects revenge, aggression, and retaliation. The foundation of such a method is love."

Should I Confront My Offender?

Confrontation is not always wise. Confronting an unrepentant offender can lead to more hurt and delay the healing process. Sometimes we think that confronting the one who has betrayed us and forcing them to acknowledge what they have done and how it has affected us is going to give us the closure we crave. We cannot force remorse; it has to come naturally and from the heart. Even if we get a forced apology, it's not going to mean anything because it wasn't sincere. Years ago, a friend offended me and refused to apologize. It's either that she truly didn't realize or maybe she just didn't want to see what she had done wrong. Whatever the case, when I confronted her and asked for an apology, she refused! After going back and forth with her for what seemed like an eternity, she finally apologized. That is called a forced apology. I never accepted it because it wasn't sincere! If someone is truly sorry about what they have done, you shouldn't have to beat it out of them. Her total lack of remorse eventually destroyed the relationship, and we never reconciled. I forgave her, as if she hadn't apologized, because in fact she hadn't. The apology was forced and a forced apology is no apology at all. The Bible says, "Out of the abundance of the heart the mouth speaks" (Matt. 12:34). If the offender's heart is truly repentant, we wouldn't have to ask or force an apology for bad behavior.

Pray for Your Enemies

Have you ever prayed for someone that has offended you? I have! And it was one of the hardest things to do. One time, I was praying about someone that had hurt me, and while I was praying, I felt God told me to pray a blessing upon that person's life. I just about had a heart attack when I heard it. I said, "God, you can't be serious. Do you have any idea what this person did to me? Why are you asking me to pray a blessing upon his life?" The very thought of praying for someone that had broken my heart was absurd! I told God that I wasn't there yet. To me, it was like God asking me to pray for the devil. I felt that if I was honest and up front with God by admitting that I wasn't at that place of maturity yet, God would understand why I couldn't do it. Wrong! The fact of the matter was I didn't want God to bless this person. I probably would have choked on my words if I had been obedient then.

Several months later, I was reading a book called *Free Yourself to Love* by Jackie Kendall. The author was talking about the same thing—praying for our enemies. Again, I heard the same still, small voice of God telling me to pray a blessing upon this person. This time, I was a lot more receptive! Honestly, I still wasn't ready! But at least, I was cooperative. I put down the book, went into the bathroom, and wept! I didn't want to disappoint God again, but I honestly didn't know what to pray about, so I ask God. It took every ounce of strength that I possessed to open up my mouth and say the words.

I wept indignantly as I brought my flesh under subjection to the will of God. I didn't want to do it because God wanted me to. I didn't want to echo empty meaningless words. I wanted my love for God and my willingness to please Him to take precedence over wanting to see this person suffer like I had suffered. Reluctantly, I finally asked God what to pray for, and He told me three things. First, to pray for this person's relationship with his son, that God would heal the rift between them and bring peace. Second, his business, that God would bless the fruits of his labor and increase him. Last but not least, that God would speak to him about what he had done to me. After I prayed the blessing, I washed my face, combed my hair, and left the bathroom, knowing that I had done the will of God.

Mahatma Gandhi said, "The weak can never forgive. Forgiveness is an attribute of the strong." If you can pray a blessing upon someone that has hurt you, then you are a lot stronger than you think. When God tells us that we are to pray for our enemies, He doesn't expect us to do it in our own strength. He knows that it's more human for us to pray a cursing over them than a blessing. God is looking for a heart that will be obedient to Him no matter what. He wants us to do it more for ourselves than for our enemies. God knows the moment we are obedient to do His will, it is in the act of obedience that our freedom will come. Yes! Our enemies will benefit from our prayers, but we will benefit even more. Look at Job in Job 42:10 (NKJ). "And the Lord restored Job's losses when he prayed for his friends. Indeed, the Lord gave Job twice as much as he had before." Job's prayer of blessing for his three foolish friends prevented God from taking vengeance upon them for what they had done to Job.

There is a lesson to be learned from this. When we pray for those who have hurt us, we're actually asking God to reserve judgment and not to give them what they truly deserve. By showing our act of kindness, it proves to God that our love for Him is greater than our hatred for our enemies. We see it again in the life of Moses. When Moses' sister, Miriam, and his brother, Aaron, sinned against him, Moses prayed for them, and God spared their lives. Jackie Kendall, author of *Free Yourself to Love*, said, "The forgiveness tool of praying a blessing is not a magic incantation. It is a fortifying tool for the one who desires to forgive effectively. This is not a tool with which we can manipulate God or other people; rather, using it aligns our hearts with the heart of the Great Forgiver. This tool allows you to strengthen your identity as one who forgives—and free yourself to love."

I Need Closure

The one thing that bothered me the most about losing my friend, the one that rejected me after twenty-five years of friendship, was the silence. I never thought for one second that the friendship was invincible because nothing is unbreakable—only the love of God. It was the silence that hurt the most. Martin Luther King Jr. said, "In the end, we will remember not the words of our enemies, but the silence of our friends." My best friend just walked away without saying one word. It was the total disregard for my feelings that pained me. It took three years to find closure and to move past the pain of rejection. Even though I had made the decision to forgive years ago, I had to give God time to take me through the natural process of healing.

Unfortunately, heart wounds are the hardest to heal. A broken heart is not the same as a broken leg. You can't put a cast on your heart for a couple of months and it's healed. It can take a lifetime for a broken heart to mend, and even then, it's going to leave scars. Rose Kennedy said, "It has been said, 'time heals all wounds.' I do not agree. The wounds remain. In time, the mind, protecting its sanity, covers them with scar tissue and the pain lessens. But it is never gone." I agree with Rose Kennedy. Time will lessen the pain. But in my opinion, only God can truly heal a broken heart. And even so, He does it over time! For most people, closure usually comes after an apology. To hear someone that has hurt you say "I am sorry" brings a sense of closure that is often needed after we have been hurt. But in my case, it wasn't going to happen anytime in the near future, and I didn't want to waste any more time waiting for it.

There is a common misconception about forgiveness and reconciliation that is associated with an apology. Most people can't move forward or achieve forgiveness until they have received an apology. For the wounded heart, an apology is like medicine. I was one of those people that couldn't move forward unless I got an apology. Not that the offense had to be great but for the fact that I needed to hear those words or else I would get stuck, stuck in unforgiveness—rehearsing the offense over and over in my mind. We don't need an apology in order to find closure. Once we have made a decision to forgive, we will find the closure that we need and the freedom to free ourselves to love.

Repeat Offenses

What happens when the one who hurt you keeps hurting you over and over again? There are two kinds of repeat offenders. (1) The coward. This kind of repeat offender truly desires to make amends, but they're afraid. They are fully cognizant of their sins and perhaps genuinely repentant, but they don't possess the courage to face the people they have hurt. In a bolder term, they're cowards! They're terrified of the possibility of rejection. This person knows that in order for them to ask for forgiveness, they have to humble themselves, which makes them vulnerable to rejection. This individual would much rather not say anything at all than to risk being offended by the same person they have offended. (2) The proud. This kind of offender is the deadliest! They are too proud to ever admit when they are wrong! They too are fully cognizant of what they have done, but they will never admit it! And if they can't admit it, then they will never apologize. The Bible says, "God resists the proud, but gives grace to the humble" (1 Pet 5:5). Pride is a terrible thing. It's a sin!

Repeat Offender 1 (The Coward)

My friend of twenty-five years, the one I spoke about earlier in this chapter, is a very good example of repeat offender 1. After three years of silence, he finally came back. I was stunned when I picked up the telephone—three years later—to hear his voice on the other end of the line. It was as if time had stood still, but it hadn't! During those three years, I went through hell trying to deal with the pain of rejection. Then, he came back and didn't even offer one word of an apology. That was the second time he had rejected me. The first time, he stayed away for ten years and just suddenly reappeared without so much as one word of apology. I forgave him the first time without the apology, and we reconciled. That's why he thought he could do it again and get away with it. Because he had!

Repeat offenders prey on your ability to forgive easily and unconditionally! It's nothing for them to hurt you and turn around and abuse your generosity. They are oblivious to the kind of pain they have inflicted, and the scars they leave behind are indelibly etched in the minds of those they have hurt. After all the years that had passed between my friend and I, it still amazes me that he has the audacity to come back and just try to pretend that he didn't hurt me. It's incomprehensible how these people can justify hurting others, especially the ones they claim to love, and find a way to sleep at nights! It's absurd!

Repeat Offender 2 (The Proud)

I have a brother that is an infamous repeat offender 2. This brother keeps doing the same things over and over again to hurt me, and he has not—yet—offered one word of an apology. It's like he has no remorse whatsoever! Every time I spoke to him about his bad behavior, it's like talking to a two-year-old in a forty-five-year-old's body. Finally, I just got fed up and separated myself from him. Before I did, I wrote a letter to him outlining his habitual offenses and his blatant lack of remorse. I explained in length how appalled I was with his behavior and that it would be in my best interest to separate from him. As much as it pained me to cut off my own brother, he left me with no other recourse. This brother and I live in different countries, so we communicate predominantly by telephone.

After the last incident, I changed my telephone number and cease all communications with him. I hadn't spoken to him in over a year before he tracked me down and called me. When I spoke to him for the first time, he offered no explanations or apologies as always. He didn't even address what had happened at all. I guess, in his mind, he hadn't done anything. He hadn't changed one bit! My letter hadn't moved him an inch. He was just as unrepentant as he had always been! He jumped back into my life with both feet planted and picked up where he left off as if nothing had happened. He was not going to say those three little words I wanted to hear in order to heal the relationship, and I couldn't keep enabling him to continue abusing me habitually.

I had to make a decision to forgive without getting an apology, but I also had to put an end to his abusive behavior. And the only way I could have done it was to stop putting any expectations on him whatsoever. Sometimes we're not going to hear the words "I am sorry" from the people that have offended us. Unfortunately some people don't have it in them to humble themselves and do the right thing. We have to leave them to God, and He will humble them for us. But it doesn't mean that because we have chosen to do the right thing by forgiving repeatedly without an apology, we should allow people to keep victimizing us. We have to put a stop to them! We owe it to ourselves to break the cycle of abuse.

Jackie Kendall, author of *Free Yourself to Love*, said, "Our level of frustration with people's offenses is directly proportionate to our expectations of their behavior. Indeed, my own expectations set the very framework for my being offended again. And while life provides predictable trouble, God provides equally predictable vouchers of grace." If the offender refuses to do the right thing, by all means, separate yourself from them if you feel that it's the only recourse you have. You have the God-given right! William Shakespeare said, "He who has injured thee was either stronger or weaker than thee. If weaker, spare him; if stronger, spare thyself."

I chose not to separate myself from my brother again, only because he's my brother. But I chose to spare myself by not putting any expectations on him. This way, I finally freed myself to love him unconditionally! There's an old Jamaican saying that goes like this, "You can't squeeze blood out of a stone." In other words, it would be futile for me to keep placing unrealistic expectations on my brother, knowing that he cannot or refuses to meet them. Family is important to me, and if I can find a way to live in peace with him, I will! To truly have the heart of Christ is to let His mind be in me.

A Hole in the Wall

When you hurt someone, it is your responsibility to make it right! You have to go to that person and ask forgiveness. You cannot justify your bad behavior by compounding the hurt with pride or cowardice. Pride goes before the fall! Even if you have to write a letter of apology, it's better than silence! You have to say those three little words, "I am sorry." After many years of repeated offenses, I never heard those three little words from my brother or my friend, and maybe, I never will! I heard a story about the dangers of repeated offenses that moved me. It was about a teenager that kept getting into trouble and constantly apologizing for it. No matter how much he kept hurting his parents, he would turn around and do something else to hurt them—knowing that they loved him and he would be forgiven.

One day, his dad took him out to the garage for a talk. Dad picked up a hammer and drove a nail into the garage wall. Then he handed the hammer to his son and asked him to pull out the nail, leaving a hole in the wall. Dad went on to explain to his son that every time he did something to hurt them, it was like driving a nail into their hearts. But every time they forgave him, it was like pulling the nail out. Then the father asked his son to use the hammer to pull out the nail hole out of the wall. The boy told his father that it was impossible to do so. The story illustrates the consequences of repeated offenses. Even after we have received forgiveness, the scars from each offense still remain.

Reconciliation

Reconciliation can be a wonderful experience, but only if God is behind it. Not all relationships are reconcilable! When we are considering reconciliation after a major betrayal, we have to pray and ask God if reconciliation in certain situation is right for us. Just recently, at a funeral of all places, I ran into an old friend that had rejected me over ten years ago. I know that funerals and weddings have a way of bringing out the best in people, but what was about to happen came as a total surprise. Sad to say, I had attended the funeral service for a fifteen-year-old boy that had committed suicide.

He was the son of one of the most wonderful Christian couples I know. The sudden, senseless death of their son had turned the community into a pool of grief. The day of the funeral, the church was packed, including the overflow rooms. Teenagers from the high school, where the boy had attended, members of the local church, where the family worshipped, along with neighbors and friends joined together to mourn the loss of someone so young, someone that died too soon. The sounds of wailing echoed throughout the building and floated out into the street. It was unlike anything I had ever seen or heard. To see the tremendous outpouring of love and support of an entire community demonstrated at the funeral that day was astounding!

After the service was over, an old friend approached me and asked for my telephone number. At first, I was a little apprehensive. I wasn't sure what to make of it seeing that our friendship was long over and had been for more than ten years. But my curiosity got the better of me, and I gave it to her. This woman and I were extremely close friends for many years. We were like sisters. I met her through one of my sisters who had befriended her first. Come to think of it, we met at her baby shower, and I was immediately drawn to her. We became friends in a relatively short time, and I loved her dearly. She was one of those people that you meet and, within a short time, you feel like you've known this person your entire life.

So when the friendship fell apart for reasons unbeknown to me, it broke my heart. I did everything within my power to salvage the relationship, but she just didn't want anything to do with me at all. No matter how many times I asked her what was wrong, she never told me. I prayed fervently, almost every day, for three years, for God to restore the friendship, but He never did. After a while, I finally gave up. I remember the exact day when I realized for the first time that the friendship was really over.

It was a Sunday afternoon, and we had just left church and was on our way home. My husband and I were talking in the car about an incident that had just happened in church, and clearly, he saw that I was a little perturbed and wanted to do something to calm my nerve. Being the thoughtful man that he is, he stopped at a coffee shop to get me a cup of coffee. Thank God for caffeine, it works every time! As soon as my husband and children exited the vehicle and went inside the coffee shop, I heard the still, small voice of God say, "I want you to let go and stop trying." I knew immediately what He meant, and I made the decision that day to let go.

Before that day, Sunday mornings were the hardest for me. I hated going to church. All my life, church represented a place of peace, but it wasn't like that anymore. It got to the point where I didn't want to attend that church anymore. I know how foolish that must sound, but I almost left a church that I got married and dedicated my children in, a church that I loved all because someone wasn't talking to me. Unbelievable! God showed me that running away from our problems wasn't the answer—forgiveness was! So again, I had to make the decision to forgive someone that had hurt me deeply without hearing those three little words, "I am sorry." Up to this point, it was starting to become habitual.

Then all of a sudden, after ten years of not knowing what had happened and why she ended the friendship, she wanted to meet with me over coffee. By then, I was starting to notice a pattern of losing friends for reasons unbeknown to me. It had been going on for such a long time that I just accepted the fact that there was something terribly wrong with me why my friends were rejecting me. But I was wrong! There was nothing wrong with me at all. There was a stronghold in my relationships, and I wasn't aware of it.

A stronghold is something familiar that keeps happening to us over and over again. And strongholds aren't easily broken. First, we have to identify them and then we have to pluck them up by the root. But the only way to do that is with fasting, prayer, and by using the word of God consistently until the pattern breaks. A stronghold is something that the devil uses to tear us down and keep us from living the life that God wants you to live. I had a stronghold that was tearing apart my relationships, and I had to put a stop to it. I had to take authority over it and pluck it up by the root. Even though I had forgiven this woman and had moved on a long time ago, we still hadn't reconciled our differences.

Reconciliation can only be achieved when the offended person receives and accepts an apology, and the relationship is restored. Reconciliation cannot be achieved unless there is an apology. Let me clarify it for you. We don't need to get an apology in order to establish forgiveness, but we have to get an apology before reconciliation can take place. Fortunately, in the end, she apologized, and I accepted. That is why I can safely say that we have completely reconciled our differences. To be reconciled with someone doesn't always mean that we have to go back to the way things were. Most of the time, we can't just pick up from where we've left off. It's not that simple! Reconciliation simply means that the individuals involved are no longer separated by a dispute or a hurt. And it doesn't necessarily mean that the relationship has to start over either. Things change, and people change too.

Sometimes these individuals can outgrow one another, which make it hard to reconnect again. This woman and I don't have the same relationship that we had before—that's not possible! We are no longer the same two people that we were before we separated. In my opinion, the relationship that we had didn't work. That's why it ended. But the relationship that we have now is a work in progress. I would like to believe that we are a lot wiser today than we were yesterday. I remember the day when we met for coffee and talked. At first, we were both guarded. We were both a little uncomfortable with one another, but the more we talked, I could clearly feel the walls between us lowering slowly as we were reminiscing about the past. It was like slowly sipping a glass of my favorite wine, trying to savor every moment of it.

We talked for hours about our lives and where we had been for the past ten years. Then all of a sudden, she started to cry as she poured out her heart about how sorry she felt about hurting me and why she ended the friendship. After finally learning the truth after ten years, I burst into tears and wept bitterly! We fell upon one another's neck and sobbed with great remorse for all the years that we had foolishly lost over something so trivial.

Only if she had confided in me and told me what was happening inside of her heart. I might have been able to save the friendship. It was the most honest, sincere, and heartfelt pouring out of affection I had ever experienced. Her apology moved me to tears. She asked if I would be willing to try and put the friendship back together again and I said yes. Although we have both changed significantly over the ten years that we weren't friends, I knew in my heart that it was God that brought us back together again. Every day, I look forward to the both of us rediscovering one another in a new way. Now, we don't talk a lot on the telephone or even see each other more than once in a while, but whenever we run into each other at church or at the hairdresser, we hug each other as if we haven't seen one another in decades. We take full advantage of the moment and make every second count until we see each other again. I thank God for restoring this friendship because I had truly missed my dear friend.

Unfortunately, in some cases, there are relationships where reconciliation is not always a healthy step. Sometimes separation between you and the person that has hurt you is necessary, so don't always look to God to put the friendship back together. It may not be in your best interest. If you're waiting on God to bring reconciliation between you and someone, and you've been waiting for a very long time and it still hasn't happened, let me encourage you to relinquish it into God's hands. He knows what's best for everyone involved. Not all relationships are reconcilable. Some are irreconcilable and should remain that way.

Here is one example of a relationship where God usually doesn't bring reconciliation. In my opinion, I don't believe that God would bring reconciliation in a relationship where some type of sexual abuse was involved. The man that molested me when I was seven years old still hasn't apologized to me even after forty-four years. And even if he does, I still don't expect God to bring reconciliation between him and me. What could I possibly gain by having this person back into my life? Since I have already forgiven him and I am no longer his victim, what could either one of us benefit from having any kind of a relationship? Some people are far better off not having any kind of a relationship with an offender, especially repeat offenders. Situations like those can be detrimental. Sure, I would have loved to hear, "I am sorry" from this man especially because I see him every time I go to Jamaica to visit my father. But I don't need it anymore. I have forgiven him without the apology, and that's all God required of me. The Bible says, "Owe no one anything except to love one another, for he who loves another has fulfilled the law" (Rom. 13:8).

Now, I have heard of cases where God has brought reconciliation in physical and emotional abuse relationships, but never a sexual one. I know a man that was being physically abused by his wife for many years, and God healed their relationship and saved the marriage. This man was a husband and father that had suffered silently for many years. He never confided in anyone, except to me. Nobody knew what was going on behind closed doors. He was too ashamed and thought that his family and friends would have looked upon him as being a weakling. His wife had a nasty temper, and every time they had a disagreement, she would attack him physically. He told me that as much as he wanted to knock her out, he didn't because he was taught not to hit women.

What was hard to believe when he finally opened up and confided in me was that he felt that his wife really loved him, but she just didn't know how to control her temper. Because she was a victim of domestic violence when she was a young woman, she became an offender, which was something that she truly loathed. Somehow, this woman went from being a victim to becoming an abuser. Fortunately, her husband recognized that she really didn't want to do the things that she had been doing, and he forgave her and stayed in the marriage until God finally healed her.

It's Never Too Late to Say, "I am Sorry"

In 1983, after my father walked me down the aisle and gave me away at my wedding, he packed his things and walked out on his wife (my mother) and children. Six months prior to my wedding, my father and I were in the mall shopping for one of his numerous ritualistic trips to Jamaica when he announced to me that he was planning to leave my mother. My wedding date was originally set for sometime in June 1984, but my father told me that if I wanted him to give me away at my wedding, I better change my date to sometime that same year. I had just gotten engaged and had planned on a one-year engagement to give my fiancé and I time to save our money for a proper wedding. Now, I was being forced to move up the wedding date, six months earlier, if I wanted my father to walk me down the aisle. Of course I wanted my father to walk me down the aisle! What woman doesn't? I was upset! What kind of a father would tell his child that he was going to leave her mother for another woman? He told me that he had done enough for my mother and her children and that I should take over now.

I was twenty-four years old and was engaged to be married. I was getting ready to move out of my parents' house to start a new life for myself. Now, my father was telling, not asking, me to assume his responsibilities as a husband and father. It felt like someone had just plunged a knife into my heart. I desperately wanted to break down and cry at that moment, but I couldn't! I was in the mall. In those days, my father would travel to Jamaica, at least four or five times a year, to visit his girlfriend and the six children that he had with her. Because he didn't know how to shop for women and children's clothing, he would ask me to go with him to buy clothes for the woman and children that he eventually left my mother for. I never fully understood what kind of a hold my father had on me because I would have done anything for him.

My father meant every word of what he said to me that day in the mall. After he walked me down the aisle at my wedding on December 3, 1983, my father abandoned my mother and two minor children. He left my brother who was sixteen and my sister who was twelve. He took everything and the kitchen sink when he left. He cleaned out the bank accounts, shipped the two vehicles that we had, and left my mother penniless. At that time, my mother had been a homemaker for many years, but after my father left, she had to find a job to support herself and her two children. I helped her to get a job at the company where I was working. So my mother, my older brother, my husband and I remained in the house and paid the mortgage. Three years later, my father came back and demanded his share of the house, forcing us to either buy him out or put up the house for sale. We didn't have enough money to buy out his share, so we had to put up the house for sale.

After the house was sold and we moved into an apartment, my mother foolishly allowed him to stay with us until the paperwork from the sale of the house had gone through. Despite how badly my father had treated my mother, she still showed him compassion. My mother received half and my father received half from the proceeds of the sale of the house, but still, that wasn't good enough for my father. He wanted more. He wanted more of my mother's half, so he manipulated one of my brothers to borrow money from my mother and give it to him. Unbeknown to my mother, she loaned the money to my brother, and she never got it back even to this day.

Over the years, I kept in touch with my father. I still have a fairly close relationship with him in spite of how poorly he treated my mother. He did some unforgiveable things to his family, but I still love him and I have forgiven him. It would be twenty-six years after my father walked out on my mother before he finally apologized to her for all the heartache and pain that he caused her. He waited until he was an old man before he humbled himself and said those three little words "I am sorry" Imagine waiting twenty-six years for an apology. Fortunately for her, my mother had already forgiven him long before that. She did what God told her to do. She forgave him without ever knowing if he would say those three little words. Although he apologized to her, my parents' marriage was never restored. Now, they are well into their seventies, and they talk on the telephone occasionally, but they are not friends.

My mother is an amazing woman. She is my hero! She put up with a whole lot over the years for the sake of her six children. She knew that my father had fathered over twenty children with at least four women, but she stayed in the marriage to ensure that her children had a roof over our heads and food on the table. And we always had. That was one thing my father made sure of until he finally left. He may not have been a good father in a lot of ways, but in his own dysfunctional mind, I believe that he actually thought that he was a good father. I think that he thought that being a good father was making sure that his children don't go to bed hungry. But being a good parent is a more than that.

Its being a good role model and doing the best that you can to always put your children's welfare and safety first. It's putting their needs above your own until they become adults. And even then, a good parent is always there, if they can, even when their children become parents of their own. I cannot count all the times I turned to my mother for help even though I am married and have children of my own. And she never turned me away. She has been a wonderful mother, grandmother, and now, a great grandmother. For a tiny woman that stands barely four feet and a couple of inches tall, she is the biggest woman that I know. She is truly a great woman of Zion.

An old friend

Talking about waiting years for an apology, this reminds me of a man that I was friendly with when I was about sixteen years old. We were only friends—at least on my part. We never dated. Regardless of that, I knew deep down in my heart that he felt more and he wanted more. Unfortunately, I never looked upon him that way. Even though he was a kind, sweet, young man, he was just my friend. About a year later, one of his friends swept me off of my feet, and we started dating. My actions wounded this man. In his mind, he thought that maybe, one day, he and I would become more than just friends, but when I started dating one of his friends, he realized that it wasn't going to happen. Sometimes, we make the dumbest decisions and our actions hurt others for a lifetime. The friendship ended abruptly and he never spoke to me again. I never thought to apologize to him for dating one of his friends because we were never lovers! In my mind, I didn't do anything wrong!

Over thirty years later, one day, just an ordinary day . . . nothing special, I was sitting at the dining room table having breakfast when suddenly, I heard the voice of God said, "You owe Ben an apology." (His real name is not Ben) I replied, "Ben! I owe Ben an apology— for what?" God told me that Ben was deeply hurt by me rejecting him for one of his friends. He told me that Ben was still carrying around all that hurt and rejection even after thirty years. When I heard that, you could have knocked me over with a feather. I knew that this man, Ben, never spoke to me again after I started dating his friend. Whenever our paths would cross, either at a party or at a mutual friend's house, he would shy away or just find an excuse to leave.

I may have been young and naïve back then, but I never thought that I owed him an apology. It wasn't as if I was his girlfriend and I cheated on him with one of his friends. Yes—I knew that he was hurt by us not being more than just friends, but I thought that he had gotten over it a long time ago. It never dawned on me that he was consumed with unforgiveness towards me, especially after thirty years. I ask God to set up a meeting between Ben and me, so that I could apologize to him. At that time, I had no idea where or how to find him. But, if it was truly God that had spoken to me, then—it wasn't my responsibility to find Ben, it was God's. If you want to know the mind of God concerning something in your life—just ask Him and then step back! About a week later, one of my friends called me up and invited me to meet him for coffee.

He was downtown shopping in the market and asks if I could meet him at a nearby coffee shop. Normally, I wouldn't have gone to that coffee because it was out of my way. I left my house that day thinking that I was going to meet my friend for coffee, but God had something else in mind. It was a date with Ben, and God was the matchmaker. I arrived at the coffee shop early and thought that I should just go ahead and order my food. I was standing in line patiently waiting for my turn to place my order when I heard the voice of God whispered into my spirit to turn around. I gently turned to see what was so relevant for God to bid me to see, only to find a familiar stranger standing directly behind me. It was Ben. When he saw me, the look upon his face was priceless! It was as if he had seen a ghost. Up to that point, I hadn't seen him in over thirty years.

We both acknowledged one another and I proceeded to the counter to place my order. I knew right away that God had arranged this meeting and it was the opportunity that I had asked for to right the wrong that I had done to Ben. After I picked up my order, I went back to him and ask if I could have a word with him after he was finished. He agreed. I was seated at a table when he approached me. I invited him to sit down for a minute and he did. I needed to tell him what I had in my heart before my coffee companion arrived. I apologized to him after thirty years had passed for hurting him, and as I was pouring out my heart to him, I could see the tears in his eyes, as if he had waited a lifetime to hear me say those three little words, "I am sorry."

When I saw how much it meant to him and the tears that were in his eyes, I knew for sure—beyond a shadow of a doubt that it was God who had arranged the meeting after thirty years. God will recompense his children even if it takes thirty years to do so. Ben was stuck in unforgiveness. He didn't know how to forgive me without an apology and God knew that. I may have been totally oblivious to what was going on in Ben's heart, but God wasn't! I needed to apologize and I was happy to do so. What would have happened if I was disobedient by not apologizing? I think that I would have done myself a grave injustice. It's one thing to be ignorant, God will understand and even pardon our ignorance, but it's another thing to be blatantly disobedient.

When God takes the time to show us the error of our ways, it's important that we listen and obey. I believe that if we don't, then there are consequences for our actions—or lack thereof. If I had known about Ben's inability to move forward because of what I had done, I would have apologized a lot sooner. God hates pride. And that's the problem with a lot of us. We don't know how to humble ourselves and do the right thing—even after we know in our hearts that we have done wrong. Prolonging the inevitable is foolish!

Remember the Pain!

I wrote this saying, "Remember the pain," on a small piece of Post-it paper and stuck it unto my bedroom mirror. My thirteen-year-old son Philip came into my bedroom and saw the piece of paper and said, "Mommy, what's that?" pointing to the piece of paper on the mirror. I explained to him that it was a reminder to me not to keep making the same mistakes over and over again. He laughed and said, "Mommy, that's a good idea. I think that you're just too nice! You keep letting people run all over you." Even my thirteen-year-old sees it for what it is. We need to remember the hurt when someone betrays us, especially when the hurt is deep. By keeping the memory of the betrayal in the forefront of our minds, we will learn not to keep putting our hand in the fire. Not because we have forgiven means that we have forgotten.

God Doesn't Waste Anything

Jackie Kendall, author of *Say Goodbye to Shame*, talked about the sudden back-to-back death of her sister and father, both within a year of one another. During her time of grief, God used a dear friend of hers to speak love and comfort into her heart. Jackie shared the words of encouragement that God gave her this way, "Jackie, I am going to plant a garden in the center of your pain, a garden that will bless not only your life but also the lives of many others." Out of the death of Jackie's sister and father, something beautiful happened. God did the same thing for me too. When my friend rejected me, it was my mother who encouraged me to keep a journal of my sufferings. From that journal came the contents of this book. Indeed, God doesn't waste anything! Especially not our sufferings! God used the pain of rejection from my friend and planted a garden in the center of my pain. This book is the garden that God planted in the midst of my sufferings. It has been said, "Life has to be lived in a forward motion but can only be understood by looking back. This demands that we trust in the loving purposes of a sovereign God. We must trust that He is in control—especially when life seems to be out of control."

In Genesis 41:51, 52, Joseph had two sons. He named the firstborn son, Manasseh, which means, "For God has made me forget all my toil and all my father's house. And the name of the second he called Ephraim, which means, "For God has caused me to be fruitful in the land of my affliction." Only God can cause us to be fruitful in our sufferings—like Joseph. In Genesis 48, after Joseph was reconciled with his family, he brought his two sons, Manasseh and Ephraim, to Jacob, his father, and the children's grandfather, for Jacob to bless them before he dies. As it was their custom, Joseph carefully positioned his two sons in the order of their birth. He placed Jacob's right hand on Manasseh, the eldest son's head and his left hand on Ephraim, the youngest son's head.

But surprisingly, Jacob crossed his arms deliberately and put his right hand on Ephraim's head. Jacob purposefully went against tradition and blessed the younger son above the eldest. This displeased Joseph because he knew the significance of what had just happened. When Joseph confronted Jacob about what he had done, this is what Jacob said, "I know, my son, I know. He also shall become a people, and he also shall be great; but truly his younger brother shall be greater than he, and his descendants shall become a multitude of nations."

It was a repeat performance of what had happened to Jacob when he was a child. In Genesis 27, Jacob had a twin brother name, Esau, but Esau came first, which made him the eldest. But because Rebekah, their mother, favored Jacob over Esau, she did the exact thing that Jacob did when it came time for their father, Isaac, to bless them. The only difference is that Isaac didn't cross his arms on purpose. He was deceived by his wife, Rebekah, and his son, Jacob, into blessing Jacob first rather than Esau. History had repeated itself. The blessings that rightfully belonged to Manasseh, Joseph's firstborn son, were given knowingly to his second son, Ephraim. When I read the story for the first time, I was hung up on the irony of history repeating itself. I wasn't looking at why Jacob went against tradition to bless Ephraim over Manasseh. The name Manasseh means "for God has made me forget all my toil and all my father's house." What Jacob was saying by blessing the younger over the eldest is that it's much more profitable to produce fruits in your sufferings rather than to forget them.

God doesn't want us to forget where we have been. He wants us to remember our mistakes, failures, disappointments and pains so that we can learn from them. Getting over a painful past is a great achievement, but producing fruits through the hard times is greater! If it hadn't been for my sufferings, I would have never thought about writing this book. This book would have died inside of me. And I say that literally because on October 11, 2009, I suffered a ruptured brain aneurysm two years after I started writing this book, which I will talk more about it in the next chapter.

When I lost my twins, I couldn't imagine anything positive coming from such senseless suffering. For the longest time, it felt like such a colossal waste until I met Tina. (That wasn't her real name) Tina was a beautiful young mother who was grieving the death of her firstborn baby who died at birth with congenital heart defect. We met through a mutual friend—our pastor, who had asked me to help her during the grieving process. I made arrangements to meet at Tina's apartment for coffee. On my way there, I kept rehearsing in my mind what I thought I should say or what I thought she needed to hear to help her through the grieving process, but what was about to happen was remarkable!

We sat in her living room and talked for hours as she poured out her shattered heart to a total stranger. She was trying to make sense as to why her baby boy had to die but couldn't. She was angry at the world, and the anger was like a consuming fire. She hated all pregnant women, especially her sister-in-law because she was pregnant. She couldn't even stand the thought of being in the same room with her, and she was ashamed of how she was behaving. The guilt was eating her alive. She was caught up in a whirlwind of mixed emotions that was unfamiliar to her, and she didn't know how to process what was happening to her. She was slowly turning into a monster. After I explained to her that she wasn't a bad person for not wanting to be around pregnant women and whatever she was experiencing was normal, she was grateful to have someone that empathized with her in her grief. By the time I left her apartment, I felt like I had relived the worst experience of my entire life, but it was worth it.

Over the years, there were many women like Tina and I felt blessed to be able to help women and men with their pain of loss. How could something as earth shattering as the death of two tiny babies help to bring healing to so many grieving mothers and fathers? Indeed, God doesn't waste anything! Not even our sorrows. Only God can take the worst thing that has ever happened to you and bring good out of it. Looking back now, I get this strange sense of peace, knowing that the death of my children was not in vain. If I had a chance to go back and change the outcome, would I do it? In a heartbeat! I wanted my babies, but it wasn't meant to be.

CHAPTER 8

Beauty For Ashes

> Birds sing after a storm; why shouldn't people feel as free to delight in whatever sunlight remains to them.
> —Rose Kennedy

The Brain Aneurysm

One of my favorite scriptures in the Bible is the apostle Paul's exhortation to know Christ in Philippians 3:10. "That I may know him, and the power of his resurrection, and the fellowship of his sufferings, being made conformable unto his death." I must have prayed this portion of scripture a thousand times wondering what it would actually feel like to know God in such an intimate way! Although I had heard many stories about the miracle working-power of God and had witnessed a few of my own, I wanted more! I wanted a demonstration of the resurrection power of God in my own life. I was getting tired of hearing about other people's experiences with God and reading about all the miracles that Jesus had performed in the Bible or in some modern day missionary's story in Africa or China. I wanted to see, Leslie, the crippled woman in the wheelchair at our church, get up and walk. But she didn't! She died instead. I wanted my own miracle, up close and personal, but it hadn't happen—yet.

Until October 11, 2009, the day before Thanksgiving Day, God finally showed up and gave me my very own miracle. Let me backtrack a little bit and take you to the day, exactly one year ago today, when I suffered a ruptured aneurysm. How ironic that I would wind up writing this chapter exactly one year ago today. It actually started on October 5, 2009, six days before Thanksgiving. That day was just an ordinary day, no different than any other. I had gone to the gym, like I usually did, at least five days a week. I remember greeting the girls that work behind the counter in the front of the club, struck up a brief conversation with them, as I normally did, and headed toward the change rooms, which were located in the back of the club.

I proceeded to lock up my things in one of the lockers, used the washroom, and headed back toward the front of the club, where the exercise equipments were. I placed my towel, a bottle of water, and my exercise program card on a nearby bench, put on my workout gloves, and started doing chest flies on one of the machines. Minutes into my program, just out of the blue, I suddenly had the worst headache of my entire life. It felt like someone had taken a sharp knife and plunged it into my brain. I suddenly released the cables, and the crashing sound of the weights ricocheted throughout the gym like thunder. I grabbed both sides of my head, staggered drunkenly over to the bench, where I had placed my things and sat down. Within seconds, the pain that had started in my head ran down the back of my neck and into my spine, like hot lava. The room felt like it was spinning, almost like a merry-go-round out of control and everything turned black as if I was going to faint, but I didn't. I felt nauseated and weak. *My God, what is this?* I wondered. Then the strangest thing happened afterward; I spoke these words quietly underneath my breath, "I shall not die but live and declare the work of the Lord." Now, why in the world would I even think of saying such a thing?

There I was in the middle of a crowded gym, in excruciating pain, and all I could think to say was a passage from the Bible! Most people would be screaming in agony from the kind of pain that I was in or desperately trying to get to the telephone to call 911. I, on the other hand, quoted a scripture verse from the Bible. Looking back, I'm so glad that I did. I firmly believe that saying those words, in faith, literally saved my life. The Bible said that there is life and death in the power of the tongue, and you know what, it's true! Later on, I found out from my neurosurgeon that the excruciating pain in my head was the moment the aneurysm had ruptured. And the hot lava that I felt running down my spine was blood. In that moment, I went from death unto life. Moments later, I realized that I couldn't turn my neck, so I used the telephone in the gym to call my husband to come and pick me up. I couldn't risk driving home and putting myself and others at risk by operating a vehicle in that condition.

About twenty minutes later, my husband arrived at the gym, and by then, I could hardly walk. The pain in my head, neck, shoulders, and back was daunting. Strangely enough, during the short drive home, I took a couple of pain pills that I had found in my purse, and the pain subsided a bit. I didn't think of going to the emergency room. I wrote it off as a strained a muscle. After all, I was in the gym when it happened. And up to that point, I was as healthy as a horse—so I thought! I was somewhat of a gym freak. Well, I was wrong about the pain being a strained muscle. Almost dead wrong! After six days of taking almost every pain medication that I could buy over the counter, without relief, I thought that it was time to see my doctor. Because it was a holiday weekend, Thanksgiving, and my doctor's office was closed until the following Tuesday morning, I had to do something. I was in so much pain, and the pain was getting more intolerable by the minute that I couldn't wait until Tuesday to see a doctor. By then, the pain had travelled down my spine and into my legs. I was scared! I asked my son to take me to the doctor that was on call for my doctor. While I was there, the unthinkable happened! I suffered a seizure.

I arrived early at the doctor's office. I wanted to make certain that I would be seen that day because the doctor was only seeing patients from 2:00-4:00 p.m. that afternoon. There were about twenty-three people ahead of me. Apparently, the others had the same idea that I had, but I wasn't disturbed by the lineup at all. I have learned a long time ago that long line ups are one of the God's many methods of teaching me patience. It's a habit of mine to always look for something positive in everything. Like my children always said, "Mom, don't sweat the small stuff." So whether I find myself in a long line up at the doctor's office or stuck in rush-hour traffic, I would always try to do my best to take advantage of the time rather than getting upset and flipping people off.

The world is changing, and rightly so, but I can remember a time in my life when people weren't in such a hurry going nowhere worth dying for. Things were a lot more slow paced and simple back then. We didn't have road rages or people fighting over parking spaces at the mall. Those were the good old days! I had intended on using the waiting time in the doctor's office to talk to my son about college and basketball. My son Jordan was a sophomore in college and captain of the basketball team. He was attending the same college that my daughter, Shea-Marie, had attended the year before. Both of them were sharing a two-bedroom apartment just about ninety kilometers west of the city where we lived. Both of my children had just come home for the weekend—like they had done numerous times before. But this time, unbeknown to them, their lives were going to change forever!

As parents to college students living away from home, my husband and I couldn't wait for long weekends and holidays for our children to come home for a visit. As much as we were in a hurry to see our children grow up when they were smaller and giving us one migraine after another, it was hard to let them go when they went off to college. Actually, I cried! I remembered when my eldest child, my daughter, Shea-Marie, went off to college. We just couldn't understand why she had chosen a school so far away from home. Then when we found out that the program that she wanted wasn't offered at any of the local colleges, our hearts sank in our chests. Although we knew that one day she would grow up and leave home, my husband and I thought that we would have liked a little bit more time to prepare ourselves for that day. Unfortunately, there never is, enough time I mean. No amount of time can ever prepare a parent for the day when your baby leaves home. Time goes by so quickly, and in the blink of an eye, they're gone. From kindergarten to college, life is an amazing journey full of surprises. And on that Thanksgiving weekend, God had a surprise that my family never forgot.

It didn't take that much time in the waiting room before the receptionist called my name. By then, my son had gone to the restroom, not knowing that my name was called. Within seconds after entering the examination room, I suffered a seizure. The doctor had no idea what was wrong with me when she called the paramedics because everything was happening so fast. It was sheer chaos in the doctor's office that afternoon. Everyone were on their feet trying to get a look at who was responsible for all the commotion. Everyone, including my son, was flabbergasted as they watched the paramedics burst through the front doors and rushed pass them toward the back of the office where the examination rooms were. My son was stunned when he realized that it was his mother that was creating all the excitement. He immediately identified himself as my son and was asked by the paramedics to remove my identification and insurance cards from my purse.

He told me later how petrified he was when he saw me flopping around on the floor like a fish out of water. He had never witnessed anyone having a seizure before. The paramedics questioned my son in hopes of ascertaining pertinent medical information about my health. Jordan told me how impotent he felt just standing there trying his very best to be brave as he watched them desperately trying to stabilize me. He followed the paramedics outside to the ambulance while he was calling home on his cell phone. My husband was busy preparing Thanksgiving dinner, as usual, not knowing that he was about to receive the worst phone call of his entire life. Good ole Dad, busy in the kitchen, cooking one of his famous Thanksgiving dinners. My husband is an excellent cook, husband, and father. He's a kind of "Leave it to beaver" father—just about the most wonderful man I have ever known. He dropped everything, picked up my son at the doctor's office, and went straight to the hospital. Upon arrival, they met with the emergency room doctor that had examined me, which was the bearer of more bad news.

The emergency room doctor told them that I had suffered a seizure and that he had ordered a magnetic resonance imaging (MRI) to determine the cause. My husband and son waited nervously for the test results, and while they waited, they prayed. With a million thoughts racing through their minds, but still trusting God that when the doctor comes back into the room, he's going to tell them what they wanted to hear. But when the test revealed a ruptured brain aneurysm, it was far worse than anyone had ever imagined. The diagnosis sent shock waves down their spines. The doctor's exact words to them were "Mr. Dixon, your wife is a very sick woman."

A brain aneurysm is one form of stroke. The brain gets its blood supply from arteries known as the circle of Willis. It is located at the base of the brain and is a loop of arteries that join in a circle then send branches out to all parts of the brain. These arteries deliver nutrition (glucose and oxygen) to the brain cells. The junctions where these arteries come together can form weak spots. These weak spots can balloon out and fill with blood, creating the outpunching of blood vessels known as aneurysms. These saclike areas may leak or rupture spilling blood into the surrounding tissues. Any type of hemorrhage is often life threatening. If diagnosed and treated early, the survival rates are increased. But once it ruptures, the survival rates are very low. In my case, it had ruptured, and I was bleeding into my skull six days before I suffered a seizure.

Unfortunately, the small city that we lived in have only two hospitals and neither one of them has a neurosurgeon on staff. Five telephone calls went out to the surrounding hospitals—that day. Hospitals that were equipped to do the kind of surgery that I needed to save my life. University Hospital in London, Ontario, was one of the five to receive a call, which happened to be in the same city my two children lived in at that time. University Hospital is considered to be one of the best hospitals in the world for neurosurgery. As soon as my husband heard that, he prayed and asked

God to let that hospital call first. Not even five minutes after he prayed, University Hospital called, and I was air lifted to their facility. The rest of my families were all together at my brother's house having Thanksgiving dinner and waiting patiently by the phone for an update on my condition. My husband and son hurried home, packed a little suitcase for me, and they all drove ninety kilometers west to where I was.

By the time they arrived, a second MRI was done. Surprisingly, God had worked a miracle on my behalf. The bleeding that the doctors saw on the first MRI had miraculously stopped. It was as if God had put his finger in the hole in my brain and plugged it. Because the bleeding had stopped, it gave the surgeons time to figure out what procedure was best to perform. During this time, it was vital that I remained unconscious to prevent further seizures, which could have caused more brain damage or worse—death! My family met with a team of neurosurgeons to discuss the diagnosis and treatment options.

Treatment for symptomatic aneurysm is to repair the blood vessels. Clipping and Coiling are two treatment options. Clipping is when a neurosurgeon can operate by cutting open the skull, identifying the damaged blood vessel and putting a clip across the aneurysm. This prevents blood from entering the aneurysm and causing further growth or blood leakage. Coiling is when a tube is thread through the arteries, as with an angiogram, identify the aneurysm, and fill it with coils of platinum wire or with latex. This also prevents further blood from entering the aneurysm. Both of these options have the risk of damaging the blood vessel and causing more bleeding, damaging nearby brain tissue, and causing the surrounding blood vessels to go into spasm, depriving brain tissue of blood supply and causing a stroke. I had the best neurosurgeons in Canada, and my surgery was a complete success.

After I regained consciousness, I had some speech and mobility impediments and some long—and short-term memory loss. But with the help of a speech and physiotherapist, I walked out of the hospital two weeks later, which was a miracle! All in all, I consider myself to be quite fortunate, fortunate to be alive. Brain aneurysms are deadly. About 10 percent of patients with a ruptured aneurysm die before receiving medical care. If untreated, another 50 percent will die within a month. Aside from the bleeding issues, there is a significant risk of artery spasm leading to a stroke. And to think that I actually survived a ruptured brain aneurysm is truly a miracle. I had always wanted to witness a miracle, and God gave me a front-row seat to my very own. Now, I look at life through a whole new set of lenses. And with a deeper appreciation for all I have endured in my life. There's nothing quite like a near-death experience to make you realize how truly blessed you are. I'm not saying, by any means, that I didn't love my life because I did! What I am saying is, for me, I had allowed the problems in my life to overwhelm me to the point that all I saw were the problems.

No one knows for sure what causes a brain aneurysm. Although it has been said that some aneurysms are congenital, it is now thought that they can be caused by stress. I firmly believe that my aneurysm was caused by stress, absolutely, no doubt in my mind. I say this because, for two years prior to the discovery of the aneurysm, I was under heavy emotional fire. I remember talking to my sister one day, and she urged me to find a way to handle the stress. She was deeply concerned that if I didn't find an outlet to channel all the stress, something bad was going to happen to me. She was right! Within months after she made that statement, I almost died! I don't think that most people realize the affect that stress has on our bodies. I believe stress is a major contributing factor to many of the diseases that plague our generation. I knew the tremendous amount of stress that I was under was breaking down my body slowly, but I didn't know how to stop it.

A Second Chance

I waited until it was almost too late to trust God with my problems. I waited until the stress stopped me, and almost killed me, before I did what I already knew to do. I had been in this predicament before, more times than I can count on my fingers and toes combined. God had rescued me out of troubles more times than He saved the Israelites in the Bible. Sometimes, I wonder why we think that worrying and stressing out ourselves about things we cannot change is going to solve our problems. And if we know that it doesn't, then why do we do it?

All the problems that I had before the aneurysm were the same problems I had after I woke up in the hospital one week later. But during the one week that I was unconscious, something incredible happened to me. I woke up free! Free from worries. Free from fear. I dropped everything. It was like I was carrying a huge knapsack on my back for a very long time, and all of a sudden, someone took it from me. I wasn't concerned about all the problems that I had or how I was going to solve them. I didn't care about any of that stuff anymore. All the stuff that I was carrying around in my knapsack had suddenly disappeared as if someone had stopped the clock.

And what seems so ironic is that it had to take a near-death experience to open up my eyes to the truth.

Why didn't I trust God with my problems, knowing that He was more than capable to take care of me? Why did it have to take something tragic to open up my eyes to God's sovereignty? Why do we find it so difficult to trust God with our lives? For some reason, it's more natural for us to yield to fear when things are going badly than to yield to peace by trusting God. Fear is the opposite of faith. It takes the same amount of effort to believe as it does to doubt. The difference between the two is, faith produces results and fear produces sicknesses and diseases. The human spirit is a lot more resilient than we think. You would be amazed, once threatened, how hard our spirit will fight to survive. When I was in the hospital fighting for my life, I remember thinking about all the times in my life when I wanted to die. Times when I thought that my problems were too painful for me to handle and death was the only way out. But when I was actually staring death in the face, all I wanted more than anything else in the world was to live. Be careful what you wish for! You might just get it. I didn't really want to die. I wanted the problems to go away.

Henry Blackaby, author of *Created to be God's Friend*, said, "For one to realize God is working out His eternal purpose in his life is to live with a sense of urgency. Only one life to live, and it will soon be past, and only what is done with God will last!" Henry Blackaby couldn't have said it any better. He must have been real good friends with my auntie Pearl, God rest her soul. My aunt Pearl was my mother's older sister. She always use to say, "We will only pass this way once and it's only what we do for Christ will last." She was right. She died in 2010 after she suffered a massive stroke in 2001, which left her totally incapacitated. She was hospitalized and never spoke one word or walked in nine years until she died. She was a wonderful woman of God. Full of wisdom and faith. She was the eldest of eight children. So when my mother lost her mother at the age of ten, it was my aunt Pearl that took on the role of a mother to her seven siblings even though she was only a teenager.

She eventually married and had nine children of her own. After her husband died, she raised them on her own. I had always admired my aunt Pearl. Not because she raised my own mother, but because of her unshakeable faith. She had the same unshakeable faith like Abraham had. I still remember all the wonderful stories and sayings that she told me when I was growing up. Stories that helped shaped my life in a positive way. I remember one story in particular about the time when she didn't have any money to buy food to feed her children. So she put on a pot of water to boil on the stove and knelt down and prayed.

She prayed and asked God to provide food to put in the empty pot that was already boiling on the stove. Suddenly, there was a knock at the door and when she opened it, she was amazed by what she saw. Standing in the doorway was one of her friends with a bag of groceries in her hands. At her funeral, one of her children told the same story and it moved everyone to tears. There wasn't a dry eye in the church that afternoon. Indeed, we only have one life to live, but it's only what we do for Christ will last. I still get chills down my spine every time I think that I almost died on October 11, 2009, at fifty years old. And to think that if I had died, all my hopes and dreams would have died with me.

Like most of us, there are places we still haven't seen and things we still haven't accomplish—yet. Even the writing of this book would have died with me. Whether we live to be a hundred years old and die peaceably in our sleep or we die a premature death at a tender age, we all want more time. I consider myself blessed because God gave me more time, and now, I live my life with the same sense of urgency that Henry Blackaby talked about. I have come to realize that nothing last forever. All things must come to an end—even our time on this earth. Only what we do with Christ will last forever. And everything else that we accomplish outside of Him will whither and died and be forgotten. I am not saying, by any means, that we shouldn't have our own goals and dreams and that we shouldn't strive to accomplish them because there's nothing wrong with that. But when we get to a place in our lives where God's vision for our lives supersedes our own and our eagerness to please Him is more important than the air we breathe, then and only then, can we live our lives with the assurance that God is truly working out His eternal purpose in us.

Awake at Last!

I was unconscious for one week before I woke up in the intensive care unit staring into this blinding white light like you see in the movies or hear people who have had a near-death experience talk about. And no, I didn't die and went to heaven; the light was from my neurosurgeon's little pen light thingamabob shining into my eyes. Then I heard a soft, soothing, reassuring voice behind the light call my name. The light went out, and I found myself gazing into the most adorable pair of baby blue eyes I had ever seen. They belonged to my doctor, and waking up to that sight was illusory. He was probably in his early forties, and he was gorgeous! He introduced himself, asked me a lot of questions, and proceeded to explain what had happened to me.

After he told me I was going to make a full recovery, I felt elated! To think that one minute, I was getting ready to celebrate Thanksgiving with my family and next, I was waking up from a coma. My stay in the ICU was nothing like all the other times I was hospitalized during my pregnancies. In spite of the favorable prognosis following the operation, I had a long road ahead of me, and I was frightened. I had a lot of problems with my memory, and I could barely speak or walk. One week of my life had just vanished into thin air! I couldn't remember details and events of my past. Apparently, it's not uncommon for people who have suffered trauma to the brain, depending on whether the injury is in the right or left hemisphere, to have all kinds of disabilities. Those with mobility and speech impediments require a large amount of physical and speech therapy in order to regain their motor skills. I had both a speech and physiotherapist assigned to me from the hospital.

And my champion of a husband, I always knew that he was there for the long haul in this marriage. But when he stepped up as father, mother, provider, nurse and more, he earned a whole lot more respect and admiration from everyone than he had before. While I was hospitalized, he drove hours, almost every day, and on the weekends to visit me in between his two jobs. And while he was there, he would take over the nurses' job and bathed me, make my bed, get me up to the bathroom or helped me with my physiotherapy.

Once, he even offered to wash my hair in bed, but only the nurses know how to do that. He would call the hospital every morning at 8 a.m. from work, to check in with the nurses because he wanted to know how my night went. He knew the nights were the hardest for me because sometimes the nurses would get so busy that they would forget to administer my pain medication every four hours. He would also make it a point to send his "good morning greetings" with one of the nurses to me because there were no telephones in the room.

Going Home

The day came for me to be released from the hospital, but unless I had someone to provide full-time care, which meant twenty-four hours a day, seven days a week, I wasn't going home. My daughter, Shea-Marie, volunteered to move back home to take care me. I was on medications for seizure and pain management because the pain was unbearable! The first night home from the hospital was insane! Nobody in the house slept at all. By the end of the first week, we were all suffering from sleep deprivation, especially my husband. He made up a bed for me downstairs in the living room so that I wouldn't have to climb up and down the stairs, but that didn't work.

Anywhere it was remotely comfortable to fall asleep, that's where I slept. Whether it was on the couch, on the bed, or on the floor, just as long as I would fall asleep, that's where I would remain for two, maybe three hours, if I was lucky. I had to take my pain medication every four hours even though they never lasted that long. After two hours or so, it would begin to wear off, but I couldn't take any more until after four hours. I took advantage of the two hours of relief whenever I got it, and the remaining two, I would pace the floors in agony.

My husband and daughter were the two primary caregivers taking turns relieving one another. They worked out a schedule between them, and together, they made a good team, like real professionals. My daughter, Shea-Marie, had become my rock. She did everything for me. She took on most of the responsibilities working round the clock with very little sleep. There were days when I feared that she was going to collapse from exhaustion, but she was like the little Energizer Bunny; she kept on going and going . . . And she never complained. My husband, on the other hand, has worked two jobs for the past ten years. His full-time job is from 4:00 a.m. until noon. Then he pinches a couple hours sleep and rushes off to his part-time job from 4:30 p.m. until 11:00 p.m. He has faithfully done this all these years so that I could stay at home with our children.

Sleep has always been important to my husband, and everyone in our house plays their part to ensure that he gets it uninterrupted. But after I got sick, everyone had to stay on top of him to make sure that he got the rest he needed. No matter how hard we tried to lighten his burdens, he wouldn't hear of it! As soon as the alarm went off to take my medications, he was the first one up, running down the stairs with the bottle of pills and a glass of water in his hands. We couldn't get him to understand that he needed to take care of his health because his family needed him to be healthy. After a while, we just gave up trying.

He wanted to be a vital part of my recovery process, and he was—and so much more! My family was the glue that held me together during this whole ordeal. I don't know what I would have done without them. I had my physical and speech exercises that I had to do daily, and everyone, including my twelve-year-old son Philip, pitched in. It was important that the others included Philip in their decisions and made him feel instrumental in the day-to-day routine that had to be incorporated into everyone's schedule, including Philip's.

There I was being cared for by my children and it was a humbling experience. For months my daughter and my husband bathed me, dressed me and even combed my hair. I vividly remember the first day my daughter gave me a bath, lotion my body and put me into my pajamas. She was so kind and gently as if she thought that if she were to apply too much pressure, I would break in pieces like a porcelain doll. And when I was in so much pain and she didn't know how to ease it, I saw tears in her eyes as she reached out to me and gently rubbed my back. I saw the look in her eyes many times as if to say that she would trade places with me in a heartbeat. If I sneezed, she was there wiping my nose with tissue. I was never more proud to be her mother and to know that her father and I have raised such a wonderful, compassionate and respectful young woman.

In the beginning, my family and friends prepared meals and visited often. But like most people, they are there for you in the beginning, but after a while things go back to normal. Do you notice that when someone dies everyone is there in the beginning, but after the funeral, they start disappearing? I'm the first to admit that I have been guilty of that. It's as if we think that people's lives are just going to go back to normal in a relatively short period of time after they have suffered a trauma. In the beginning, we send cards and flowers and we call and visit often. But then the cards, the flowers, the telephone calls and the visits stops.

When someone has suffered a tremendous loss, trauma or an illness, things will never go back to the way they were. Your life has changed and you will never be the same again. You will learn how to cope and eventually move beyond the pain of your circumstances, but that takes time and a lot of help from your family and friends. God bless my mother. She's an angel. I remember my father telling me that, years ago, after he left her. When I ask him why he left her if she was an angel, he said, "Because I'm a fool." My father was right. My mother is an angel and he was a fool.

My mother, the angel, visited me a lot after I came out of the hospital. She would prepare her special vegetable soups with dumplings and home-cooked Jamaican style porridges because they were my favorites. She cleaned my house, bathed me, and watched movies with me until I fell asleep on the sofa. Then she would gently cover me up and quietly disappeared into one of the bedrooms. Her heartfelt prayers and uplifting words of encouragement helped to strengthen my faith during some the darkest days of my life.

And what can I say about my big brother, Anthony. He was a constant and unwavering friend to me. God used him in such an awesome way that strengthened our relationship even more than ever. He called me a lot from work and came by often to keep me company. Sometimes he would take me out for a walk or for a drive, just to get me out of the house. He always knew when I was lonely and needed a friend and he was there, and he's still there. Tony and I had a special bond while we were growing up. We were extremely close and we still are. I thank God for giving me a friend in my brother.

Ribbons and Bows

On the other hand, my older son, Jordan, was away in college, and he wasn't handling my illness and being separated from the rest of the family, mainly me, at all. This was the son that took me to the doctor the day I suffered the seizure. He was away from home, and his feelings of isolation and helplessness during such a difficult time was upsetting for him. The pressure from school and sports was taking its toll on him. So when he came home for the Christmas holidays, he announced to everyone that he wasn't returning. We pleaded repeatedly with him about his decision to quit school, but he was adamant. As much as it pained me to watch him throw away his education and a chance of receiving a basketball scholarship, I had to take a huge step backwards to give him time to clear the cobwebs.

Jordan was a trooper. Right out the gate, he just pitched in and joined forces with the rest of the team to provide support in whatever way he could. Jordan was always the first one up in the mornings, knocking on my bedroom door, with a cup of herbal tea in his hands. He knew that there was nothing like a steaming cup of lemon and honey tea to kick-start my day. Normally, it would be a hot cup of coffee, but I wasn't permitted to have caffeine so soon after surgery. If my son didn't hear me moving around in my bedroom after 9:00 a.m., naked or clothed, he's coming in. By then, I had been out of the hospital six weeks, and the healing process was slow.

I was talking and walking a lot better, and my family doctor had finally found a better pain medication that I only had to take every twelve hours.

With the Christmas holidays approaching, I was thankful to be spending it at home with my family rather than in a cold hospital room with a bunch of strangers. To think that if God hadn't intervened and spared my life, my family would have spent the holidays grieving my death. That Christmas, my husband and children went all out with the Christmas decorations and gifts. Our house looked the best I had seen in a very long time. The Christmas lights were spectacular! I love Christmas. It's my favorite time of the year.

My friend and her two children spent the holidays with us because while everyone was celebrating the gift of my life, my friend's husband had just walked out on her and their two children. I later came to find out that he ended his marriage, of eighteen years, mainly because of what had happened to me. In the operation of his mind, he saw my near-death experience as an eye-opener for him. Apparently, he had been suffering silently for eighteen years, and suddenly had an epiphany of how precious life was and that he had been wasting away in a loveless marriage. It's amazing how some people can see a glass of water half full while others see the same glass half empty. On one hand, my family was rejoicing, but on the other hand, a very dear friend of mine was grieving.

While I was being wrapped up in red ribbons from head to toe and being presented to my family as a Christmas gift, my friend had just lost her life's partner to another woman. I just don't get it! The wrapped-up-in-red ribbons idea was mine. I wanted to give my family the best Christmas gift I had ever given them. So I came up with the idea to wrap up myself in red ribbons and bows and present myself as a gift to them. I had hoped that the miracle of my life being spared would have served as a catalyst to more miracles, but finding out that two of my friends' marriages were coming to an end as a result of what had happened to me, it was quite disconcerting. I would have preferred if my recent brush with death would have inspired others to start the business that they had been procrastinating about or to take that special trip that they had always dreamed about. But never in my wildest imaginations would I ever think that people would be ending their marriages because of me. Although I may not have been directly responsible for their decisions to end their marriages, I still feel badly that God worked a miracle on my behalf, and some people used it as a way out of their so-called loveless marriages.

It was Christmas 2009, a time of peace on earth and goodwill to all men, and I wasn't about to let anything spoil it. Everything that mattered to me in the world was all under one roof, and that was all I needed. I spent

New Year's Eve night in my own bed, wrapped up in my husband's arms, underneath a warm comforter. There wasn't one other place in the world I wanted to be more than where I was at that moment. We ushered in 2010 with new hopes and new dreams, not just only for the coming year, but for all the years we planned on spending together for the rest of our lives. I remember how corny we felt watching America on television while singing "Auld Lang Syne" to one another. It's amazing how one can find the true meaning of contentment in the simplest things.

Happy New Year!

It was January 1, 2010, I was awake most of the night, as usual, but not because it was New Year's Eve—it was the pain! When I was discharged from the hospital, I was on a drug called Dilantin for seizures and Percocet for pain. But when my family physician changed my pain medication from Percocet to OxyContin, it didn't eliminate the pain, just managed it better. I loathed taking drugs—any kind of drugs—especially one that is highly addicting like OxyContin. Whatever little sleep I got on New Year's Eve was a blessing. The next morning, New Year's Day, was quite an emotional roller-coaster ride. I was alive to see another year, and it felt fantastic! I was happy to put 2009 and all the pain that it had brought into my life behind me. Actually, 2007 and 2008 weren't much better. Everything leading up to the aneurysm was a nightmare. It was a brand-new year, and I was anxious to embrace it.

I remember sitting at the kitchen table that morning having breakfast. I was staring endlessly out the window, into the backyard, at the falling snow. By the way, I hate snow. But that morning, the fluffy, white snowflakes took my breath away. I found myself lost in the beauty of the season, the season that I had always hated. The first time I saw snow was in 1972, when I migrated to Canada from Jamaica. I was thirteen years old. Up to that point, I had never seen snow before in my entire life. I had read about it in books, heard songs sung about it, and saw it on television, but that miraculous day when my grade seven teacher gave me permission to go outside to experience it, I thought that I had died and gone to heaven. It was magnificent!

It was like slushy, but without the syrup, falling from the sky. I stood outside in awe, looking up into the sky for what felt like hours, wondering where the ice was coming from. I was already mesmerized by autumn and the stunning array of colors that I had never seen before: beautifully decorated trees and an accumulation of leaves blanketed the ground. I used to get angry when I saw people raking up the leaves and discarding them. It felt wasteful. But after many winters have come and gone, I grew to hate the winter season. I would always feel this strange sadness enveloping me whenever I watched all the signs of life fall asleep beneath the icy cold ground. The winter reminded me of what was happening in my own life for the past three years.

My life felt like it had gone to sleep for many years, and the brain aneurysm was the proverbial straw that broke the camel's back. But while sitting at that kitchen table, staring out the window on the first day of a brand-new year, God spoke to me. He told me not to fight my sufferings anymore but to embrace the journey because He was taking me some place I hadn't been before. God told me that He was going to do a new thing in my life. It reminded me of a time long ago, after I had lost the twins. God told me those exact words. At the time, I never understood it, but over the years, I kept looking for it, but it never came.

After a while, I stopped looking. But when God gives you a promise, He never goes back on His word—no matter how long it takes. After all those years, He said it again and reignited a fire of hope in my heart again. He couldn't have said it at a more imperative time in my life. My life, as I knew it, felt like it was over. I was fifty years old, and I was learning to walk and talk again. I barely remembered my life, and I felt like I was never going to be the same again. Not that the old me and my old life was all that great, but at least, it was mine.

I had already started writing this book from 2007, but I had to stop because I had lost so much of my memory after the aneurysm. I had both long—and short-term memory problems, and I couldn't very well write an autobiography if I couldn't remember much of my life. In some ways, it was fantastic. To be able to blot out all the negative things and past mistakes and hurt has some benefits. But to lose the good things and lessons learned felt like I had wasted fifty years of my life.

Who in their right mind wouldn't want to forget people who had hurt and mistreated them? Most normal people would do anything to forget the pain of their past and the people who have caused them a lot of grief. Victims of rape, child abuse, the death of a loved one or the loss of a love relationship or a friendship that ended badly. Who wouldn't want to wipe the slate clean and start all over again? But it wasn't that easy. It has been said that it's easier to understand the dark side of the moon than to understand the human brain. I was learning that the hard way—up close and personal.

Dr. Jekyll and Mr. Hyde

I have come to realize that a disease is like a lover; once it has invaded your life, your life will never be the same again. And just like you want to know everything you can about your lover, you should want to know as much as you can about your disease—I did! I did a lot of reading and still do, and I question my doctors extensively every chance I get—which is often. I made a decision when I came out of the hospital that I was going to do whatever it took to regain control of my life. As soon as I started to regain my motor skills, I read just about every material I could get my hands on about the human brain and how it operates. The human brain is so magnificently intricate; unless you are a neurosurgeon, neurologist, or a neuroscientist, etc., a regular person—like me—would find it extremely difficult to understand. I needed to understand what had happened to me and how long I was walking around with a time bomb waiting to explode inside my head. Here goes!

The human brain has two hemispheres—right and left. Jill Bolte Taylor, PhD, author of *My Stroke of Insight*, said, "The two hemispheres communicate with one another through the highway for information transfer, the corpus callosum. Although each hemisphere is unique in the specific types of information it processes, when the two hemispheres are connected to one another, they work together to generate a single seamless perception of the world." "When surgically separated, the two hemispheres function as two independent brains with unique personalities, often described as the Dr. Jekyll and Mr. Hyde phenomenon." Let's face it, the wisdom of man is great, but the wisdom of God is supreme! Man does not possess the capabilities that God possesses. Once something is broken or altered from the original state, only a sovereign God can restore it back to the original state.

Our right hemisphere controls the left half of our body function, and our left hemisphere controls the right half. My aneurysm was on the right hemisphere, which controls the left half of my body function, but it was in a very good area. I remember my neurosurgeon telling me that because it was in such a good area and the bleeding had temporarily stopped, that's the reason why they elected to do the coiling method rather than the clipping.

I had so many problems in the beginning that I really didn't care which side of my brain were responsible for them. As I had mentioned before, I had both speech and mobility impediments, long—and short-term memory loss, and a barrage of emotional problems.

All I know is that the woman who suffered a ruptured brain aneurysm on October 11, 2009, that put me in a coma for a week is not the same woman I am today. I may look the same, physically, and the sound of my voice is still distinctively my own, but the old Althea Lee Dixon is gone! With each passing day, I am becoming more of a stranger to both myself and others. With each passing day, I feel like I'm slowly disappearing and becoming someone that I don't even recognize anymore—but not all necessarily in a bad way. My body is healing at a much faster rate than my brain, and the road to recovery has become an uphill climb. Presently it has been over a year since my surgery, and in the past year, I have seen more doctors than you would see at a medical convention.

I still see my neurosurgeon, the one that operated on me. Before every visit, I have to have a MRI, at least, a week before I see him. During my visits, he goes over the results of the MRI, and I get to address whatever concerns that I have. At one of my visits, he asked me a lot of questions about my emotions and state of mind. At that time, I was just a mess. My emotions were all over the place, but I didn't know why. I was extremely depressed and suicidal. I cried every day about everything. I didn't want to leave the house, and whenever I did, I would only go out with people that I trusted.

It was then my neurosurgeon explained to me that the part of my brain that controls my emotions was affected by the aneurysm. I was placed on more medications to help regulate my emotions. I see my family doctor once a month, and she's the best. She monitors my medications and does whatever my neurosurgeon tells her to do. Then I see an oncologist every six months to monitor my white blood count because since the surgery, it has been severely low. And last but not least, I just recently started seeing a neurologist because I was still having seizures.

Six months after I was released from the hospital, my neurosurgeon instructed my family doctor to wean me off Dilantin, which was my seizure medication. He felt that since I hadn't suffered from seizures prior to the aneurysm, I shouldn't have any more. As per directed, my family doctor started weaning me off in March 2010, six months after my surgery. I was progressing well for four months. I was successfully off my seizure medication—without any incidents. Shortly afterwards, they started weaning me off OxyContin, which is for pain. I was on the road to recovery, and for the first time in months, I felt optimistic that I could actually make a full recovery. Then one day, out of the blue, I suffered another seizure and fainted on my driveway.

On the morning of the seizure, a friend, Lucian, called me up and invited me to breakfast. He was supposed to pick me up at 9:30 a.m., but when he arrived, he stayed and worked on my computer for a couple of hours until noon. So breakfast turned into lunch, and I hadn't eaten anything at all that morning. Immediately after I finished lunch, I felt sick and asked my friend to take me home. As soon as we pulled up in front of my house, I exited the car and started walking up the driveway toward the front porch. Apparently, I suffered a seizure, and luckily, my friend caught me and broke the fall. I was unconscious for a couple of seconds, and when I regained consciousness, I was lying on my front porch in my friend's arms. He called the paramedics on his cell phone, and within minutes, they arrived.

Before the paramedics arrived, my friend rang the doorbell, and when my husband opened the door and saw me lying on the front porch, his heart dropped into his stomach like a bowling ball. It was déjà vu all over again. My husband said, "When I saw her lying on the porch, I panicked! It was like I was reliving the day we found out that she had a ruptured brain aneurysm." My husband and my friend managed to get me inside the house and laid me on the sofa. Although I was conscious and coherent when the paramedics arrived, they insisted on taking me to the hospital due to my illness. This time, I was conscious during the ambulance ride, unlike the first time, and I actually had a pleasant conversation with the paramedic that took care of me until I arrived at the hospital.

I was in the emergency room for hours doing all kinds of test, including a CT scan, before the emergency room doctor confirmed that I had indeed suffered a seizure and was placed back on seizure medication. Although I didn't agree with his findings, I had to agree to take the medication intravenously that night before the doctor would discharge me. Reluctantly, I remained on the medication for about a week before I got fed up and stopped taking it. I had refused to believe that after four months off of my seizure medication, I just got up one day and had another seizure. Furthermore, I didn't feel comfortable with another doctor putting me back on medication after my own neurosurgeon had taken me off.

I elected to wait until my next checkup with my own doctor and let him instruct me what to do. Two months later, in September, I had one of my regular checkups with my neurosurgeon, and he was already notified by the emergency room doctor about what had happened and what his findings were when I was brought in that night.

My neurosurgeon referred me to a neurologist, in the same hospital, to have an EEG to determine whether or not I was still having seizures. My EEG was scheduled on November 8, 2010, followed by an appointment that same afternoon with a neurologist. The test showed that I was still having seizures—Petit Mal. This type only last a few seconds, and usually involve blank staring, fluttering eyelids, or a strange chewing motion. When someone is having a Petit Mal seizure, they may appear to be daydreaming. So thirteen months after my aneurysm, I was placed back on Dilantin to control seizures. I cannot begin to express the kind of disappointment I felt when I left the hospital that day. I felt like I had taken a giant leap backward in my health and in my life. I was distraught!

The first week back on the seizure medication was like a scene out of *The Twilight Zone*. I was so sick that I could hardly stand it. It wasn't working for me anymore, and I wasn't about to stay on it any longer even if my life depended on it. Thank God my neurologist switched me to another drug called, Apo-Clobazam, and it worked—with minimal side effects. Initially, I felt like all those months off Dilantin were a total waste.

That amazing sense of liberation that I felt when I came off Dilantin had suddenly evaporated into thin air, and the thought of living on medications for the rest of my life flooded my mind with this overwhelming sense of hopelessness. I wanted to feel normal again—that was important to me. But instead, I felt like I was living in this fantasy world that I had created in my mind. And if that wasn't bad enough, the Ministry of Transportation suspended my driver's license until my doctors can prove that I am fit to drive again. I felt like I was in a mudslide going backward, and there was nothing I could do about it.

There's a Stranger in My House

The physical rehabilitation part—that I can deal with, but the Dr. Jekyll and Mr. Hyde split personalities are crazy! Since the aneurysm, my senses have heightened tremendously. I lived in a house that has seven levels, the basement at the very bottom, and the master bedroom is on the very top. I would be lying in bed watching television in the master bedroom and can smell if there's something on the stove, in the kitchen, three levels beneath me. I can even identify exactly what is cooking. I used to smell burnt toast a lot, but I didn't know why. It wasn't until after I had suffered another seizure and was placed back on medication that I realized what was happening all along. I have read that in some cases, some people claimed to have smelled burnt toast just before having a seizure. I watched a lot of health programs on television, and I read a lot of books. You just never know when some of that information will come in handy.

I love perfumes—especially exotic fragrances. My dresser in my bedroom was covered with all kinds of fragrances until after I came home from the hospital. All of a sudden, I couldn't tolerate most of them—even my favorite ones. I became very sensitive to certain scent. They would literally make me sick. I had to give away most of them to my daughter, which made her very happy. Even my husband and children were affected by my intolerance to certain scent. My husband loves colognes and aftershaves. That was one of the many things I loved about him when we were dating. He would always have this delicious scent. But now—certain scents would just set me off, and I would literally go ballistic!

In the beginning, I practically drove everyone in my house crazy. I mean, you couldn't spray anything around me. When I was hospitalized, my neurosurgeons didn't explain to me exactly where the aneurysm was, except that it was on the right side. Nobody told me what to expect after suffering from a brain injury. So after I came home from the hospital, I didn't have a clue what was normal and what wasn't. I found out the hard way—on my own. Right off the bat, I started noticing a lot of behavioral changes. At first, I just ascribed them as a part of the side effects from all the medications that I was taking. And although the medications were responsible for a lot of the changes, the bulk of it were as a direct result of the part of my brain that was injured. I literally turned into a total stranger right before everybody's eyes—even my own. The old Althea was gone, and the new one was very complex.

It's like I had turned into this multifaceted, mysterious woman, but oddly enough, this new Althea wasn't all that bad either! Actually, she's an improvement in many ways to the old model. I had been praying for years for God to change me because I had a lot of personality flaws that needed to be changed. I know that God works in mysterious ways, but never in my wildest imagination would I ever think that God would use a brain aneurysm to change me. The old Althea was always upbeat and cheerful—always smiling—but she was the biggest pushover and a sucker for every sad story. She was kind, compassionate, and trusting. Unfortunately, some people saw my kindness and generosity as a sign of weakness and took advantage of it to bleed me dry. I was a people person—I loved people. That's one of the many reasons why people were drawn to me. I could walk into a room filled with strangers and just blend in.

I was on a first-name basis with practically everyone in the gym, hair salon, bank, doctor's office, dentist's office, etc. But as wonderful as that characteristic was, it was like a two-edged sword. It attracted all kinds of people, good, bad, and indifferent. And sometimes, it took a while to differentiate between them. By the time I figured out who is who, I would find myself constantly pulling out daggers out of my back. Now, I'm a lot more careful who I call friend. I'm not as naive and trusting as I used to be, and I don't put up with a lot of crap any more either. It's easier for me to say what I mean and mean what I say. What I'm trying to say is that I am still a people person, and I still love people, but I'm a lot more guarded. I am still kind, loving, and compassionate, but I'm a lot wiser and more balanced. Everybody keeps asking me what's wrong with me, and at first, I really thought that there was something wrong with me—but not anymore! In some ways, the aneurysm was a blessing in disguise.

I still have problems with my memory, and sometimes, I find it difficult to remember people and events from my past. Recently, I was in the change room at the gym, and this woman approached me and struck up a conversation as if she knew me. For the life of me, I had no clue who she was. She was chatting away about how long she hadn't seen me and was asking me a lot of questions about my husband and children. I couldn't place her. Her face looked familiar, but I didn't even know her name. After a while, I had to confess to her what had happened and that I had no memory of who she was. Apparently, she hadn't heard about my illness, and thank God, she wasn't offended that I didn't remember her. Actually, she was very kind and told me that she would pray for me. I'm starting to come to terms with accepting that my life, as I knew it, will never be the same again, but I take each day in stride and try to keep a positive attitude about my future.

Yet there are times when I can tell you exactly what I was wearing over thirty years ago when I first met my husband at that house party. And the irony is the people and events that I would like to forget I can't! And the things that I so desperately want to remember I can't! My memory is like a huge jigsaw puzzle with lots of missing pieces. Although my doctors have reassured me that over time, I will regain most, if not all, of my memory, somehow it doesn't reassure me, but I'm optimistic.

On the other hand, I have already started to remember details of my life that I wish would have remained lost forever. Regaining my memory is unearthing a lot of pain from my past: memories of lost friendships, lost relationships, betrayals, and abuse. Whenever I remember an abuse, whether sexual, physical, or emotional, it hurts! It's like reliving the events, and everything that goes with them all over again. And as unnerving as that may be, it's all a part of who I am. Everything that I have gone through in my entire life, whether I can remember them or not, all contributed to the woman I am today. It's all of me, the whole me—good and bad. And whatever parts of my memory I will or will not regain, I have come to accept it as a part of God's will for my life.

I have a very good support system—it's called family! And they love me—all of me. My immediate family, which is my husband and three children, has been a lifeline to me, especially since the brain aneurysm fourteen months ago. Even with the writing of this book, I wouldn't have been able to complete it without their help. They have helped me tremendously to find and fit the missing pieces of my memory that the brain aneurysm have erased. To think that I almost lost my life at the age of fifty, and if I had, this book would have died with me. For some strange reason, God saw fit to spare my life, and I'm convinced that there's still something left for me to do.

My relationship with God has grown in leaps and bounds during these trying times, but perhaps the greatest change is in my faith. I am growing in understanding the whole concept of "but without faith it is impossible to please him." I was talking with my son Jordan the other day, and he told me how different I have been since my near-death experience. He said, "Mom, not everybody has had the kind of experience with death like you've had." I replied, "What do you mean, son?" He responded, "Something definitely happened to you when you were unconscious for a whole week. You view life and the world around you differently." I completely agree with my son. I am more aware of the brevity of life and the need of how I want to use the fruitfulness of my sufferings to make a significant difference in people's lives. I read this saying written by Joe Stowell, "Life is not made by the dreams that you dream but by the choices that you make." I am in total agreement with that. This book is about all the choices that I have made and the ones that were made for me. Whether good and bad,

Years ago, I remember a friend told to me that nothing is a waste of time if it adds to the person that I am today. He was right. I am more convinced that God doesn't waste our sufferings; He uses them to mold and shape us into the kind of men and women He can use effectively as an extension of Himself. God has used the pain of every unwanted experience in my life to speak love and encouragement into the hearts of many. I have discovered that there is a tremendous anointing present when someone dares to speak up about their fears, disappointments and failures with humility and honesty. I believe that God spared my life to finish this book so that I can tell you that all things work together for our good—even the bad. To sum it all up, I have suffered tremendously doing the course of my life. But the past several years have been some of the darkest days of my entire life. Now, I feel like the darkness is fading and night is about to turn into morning.

END NOTES

Introduction

Eric Liddell (An Olympian) http://dailychristianquote.com/dcqcircumstance.html

Chapter One

1. Psalms 30:4, NKJ
2. Quote by Bruce Lee, #91 *http://www.1-love-quotes.com/love_quotes_top_100.htm*
3. Janette Oke, Love Comes Softly, Published 2003 by Bethany House Publishers
4. Genesis 19, NKJ
5. Ruth1:20, 21.NKJ
6. Book of Jonah, NKJ
7. Quote by Marie Ebner Von Eschenbach http://www.quotationspage.com/quotes/Marie_Ebner_von_Eschenbach/
8. 2 Corinthians 4:17, NKJ

Chapter Two

1. Genesis 37, NKJ
2. Genesis 41:51-52 NKJ
3. Luke 1:37 NKJ
4. Isaiah 55:8-9 NKJ
5. Isaiah 30:18 NKJ
6. John 11, NKJ
7. John 11: 25, NKJ

8. Eccl. 3:1-2 NKJ
9. Isaiah 49:15-16 NKJ
10. Genesis 18:14

Chapter three

1. Phil 3:13, NKJ

Chapter four

1. Joel 2:24, NKJ
2. Merriam-Webster's Collegiate Dictionary, 10th Ed., n "Dream" p. 351, 352
3. Paul McCartney, Yesterday (song) Wikipedia The Free Encyclopedia, Wikipedia.org/wiki/yesterday_(song
4. Abraham Lincoln, Ezine Articles. November 3, 2006 (Quoted in Ward Hill Lamon, 1911, Recollections of Abraham Lincoln, 1847-1885,) October 29, 2010
5. Merriam-Webster's Collegiate Dictionary, 10th Ed., n "Vision". p. 1316
6. Hebrews 9:27, NKJ
7. Job 33:14-17, NKJ
8. Quote by an anonymous author
9. Psalms 37:7, NKJ
10. 1 Cor 1:27, NKJ

Chapter five

1. Quote by Oliver Wendell Holmes *http://thinkexist.com/quotation/if_i_had_a_formula_for_bypassing_trouble-i_would/327085.html*
2. Merriam-Webster's Collegiate Dictionary, 10th Ed., vt "Disappoint" p.329
3. Aggerholm, Barbara. "Heart of Gold." Kitchener-Waterloo Record Thursday November 27, 2008: p E-1 and E-3
3. Heb 13:1, 2, NKJ

Chapter six

1. Phil. 4:19, NKJ
2. Matthew 26:11, NKJ
3. Matthew 26:39, NKJ
4. Phil 4:6, NKJ

5. Genesis 12:1
6. Blackaby, Henry Created to be God's friend. (Introduction) Thomas Nelson, Inc. Nashville, Tennessee, 1999
7. 1 Cor 12:9
8. Genesis 17, NKJ
9. Matthew 6:26, NKJ
10. Psalms 37:8, NKJ

Chapter seven

1. Quote by William Shakespeare http://www.goodreads.com/author/quotes/947.William_Shakespeare
2. Merriam-Webster's Collegiate Dictionary 10th Ed., v "Forgive" p. 457
3. Television program, Homecoming, ESPN, Saturday January 15, 2011 Interview with Irvin Magic Johnson
4. Merriam-Webster's Collegiate Dictionary 10th Ed., n "Relinquishment" p. 985
5. Kent, Carol. When I Lay My Isaac Down. P.53, Colorado Springs, Colorado: NavPress. 2004
6. Quotes by Martin Luther King Jr. http://www.allgreatquotes.com/martin_luther_king_day_quotes2.shtml
7. Matthew 12:34, NKJ
8. Quote by Mahatma Ghandi, http://www.money-zine.com/Career-Development/Leadership-Skill/Leadership-Quotes/
9. Job 42:10, NKJ
10. Kendall, Jackie. Free Yourself To Love. P. 181, FaithWords, Hachette Book Group, New York, 2009
11. Martin Luther King Jr. http://www.quotedb.com/quotes/46
12. Quotes by Rose Kennedy http://www.goodreads.com/author/quotes/650866.Rose_Kennedy
13. 1 peter 5:5, NKJ
14. Kendall, Jackie. Free Yourself To Love. P.184, FaithWords, Hachette Book Group, New York, 2009
15. Quote by William Shakespeare http://www.quotes.net/authors/William+Shakespeare
16. Romans 13:8, NKJ.
17. Kendall, Jackie. Say Goodbye to Shame. P. 83
18. Quote by an anonymous author
19. Genesis 41: 51, 52, NKJ

20. Genesis 48, NKJ
21. Genesis 27, NKJ

Chapter 8

1. Quote by Rose Kennedy http://www.quotationspage.com/quotes/Rose_Kennedy/ accessed on January 11,2011
2. MedicineNet.com. 1996-2010 Medicine Net,
3. Blackaby Henry, Created to be God's friend. P. 8, Thomas Nelson Inc., Nashville, Tennessee: 1999
4. Jill Bolte Taylor, PH.D. My Stroke of Insight. p.15;
5. Quote by Joe Stowell, Daily Bread, February 18, 2011.

ABOUT THE AUTHOR

Althea Lee Dixon is a wife and mother of three. Born in Jamaica, she migrated to Canada at the age of thirteen, after the sudden death of her grandmother. Althea has been a woman of faith for most of her life. She has been very active in various ministries with a passion for helping women. During the writing of this book, she suffered a brain aneurysm and almost died. But in spite of her illness which includes memory loss, speech and mobility impediments, she has successfully completed this book with the help of her family.

INDEX

A

Abraham (patriarch), 55, 134-35

B

Blackaby, Henry
  Created to be God's Friend, 135, 174
Black Terror. *See* Dixon, Raffleton
brain, human, 183
brain aneurysm, 171-73, 182, 187, 189, 195

C

clipping, 172, 183
closure, 149, 151-52
coiling, 172
corpus callosum, 183
Created to be God's Friend (Blackaby), 135, 174

D

deep sleep zone, 80
denial, 143-44
depression, 13-14, 84, 100-101
disappointments, 39, 75, 102
Dixon, Adam George, 57
Dixon, Althea Lee, 16, 105-7, 184, 195
  celebrates fiftieth birthday, 112
  celebrates twenty-fifth wedding anniversary, 99, 103
  concept of God, 28
  dreams of becoming a mother of twins, 19
  experiences hurricane in Jamaica, 116
  first pregnancy, 23, 26-27
  gets driver's license suspended, 122
  gives birth to twins, 21
  joins Mexico mission trip, 66, 129
  joins Rastafarians, 42-43, 85
  loses dream house, 58
  meets husband, 15
  migrates to Canada, 24, 181
  overcomes fear of dying, 138
  relationship with father, 28
  suffers a brain aneurysm, 11, 84, 113, 135, 166
  tries fasting, 71
  wedding heartaches, 109
Dixon, Andrew Lee, 57
Dixon, Jordan Anthony Lee, 57, 59, 61, 63, 68, 88, 131, 133, 170, 179

Dixon, Philip Jeremy Lee, 74, 116-17, 178
Dixon, Raffleton, 16, 105-6, 129, 140
Dixon, Shea-Marie Lee, 19, 100, 119, 129, 140, 170, 177
dreams
　natural, 76
　repetitive, 85-87
　spiritual, 76-78, 84-85, 99
　understanding symbols in, 100

E

Ephraim (son of Joseph), 42, 165
Esau (son of Isaac), 165
Eschenbach, Marie Ebner von, 23

F

forgiveness, 142-43, 145-46, 150, 152, 154, 156-57
Free Yourself to Love (Kendall), 150-51, 154

G

Gladys (Cyriline's twin sister), 19
God, heart of, 41
grieving, 143-44

H

Haile Selassie, 43
Holmes, Oliver Wendell, 102

I

Isaac (son of Abraham), 55, 144-45, 165

J

Jacob (son of Isaac), 39, 41, 165
Jesus Christ, 14, 29, 35, 40, 43
Johnson, Irvin Magic, 142
Jonah (prophet), 22
Jones, Jim, 43
Joseph (patriarch), 39-42, 45, 47, 78, 90-91, 165

K

Kendall, Jackie
　Free Yourself to Love, 150-51, 154
　Say Goodbye to Shame, 164
Kennedy, Rose, 151, 167
Kent, Carol
　When I Lay My Isaac Down, 144-45
King, Martin Luther Jr., 78, 87, 149, 151

L

Lazarus (friend of Jesus), 50-54
Lee, Anthony, 27, 33, 46, 121
Lee, Cyriline, 19
Lee, Jordan, 10
Lee, Mario, 52
Liddell, Eric, 14
Lincoln, Abraham, 77-79, 93, 95
Lot (nephew of Abraham), 20

M

Mad Messiah. *See* Jones, Jim
Manasseh (son of Joseph), 41, 165
Mara. *See* Naomi (mother-in-law of Ruth)
Marley, Bob, 105

Martha (sister of Lazarus), 50-52
Mary (sister of Lazarus), 50-52
Mathis, Johnny, 105, 107, 141
McCartney, Paul, 76-80
Moses (prophet), 53, 151

N

Naomi (mother-in-law of Ruth), 21, 35-37

P

Petit Mal, 186
Potiphar (servant of Pharaoh), 41
prayer, 47

R

Rachel (mother of Joseph), 39
Rastafarians, 43
reconciliation, 97, 152, 155, 157-59
repeat offenders, 152-53, 159
revenge, 41, 61, 145, 148-49
Rupert (friend of Dixon, Althea Lee), 119
Ruth (daughter-in-law of Naomi), 35-36

S

Sarah (grandmother of Dixon, Althea Lee), 19-20
Say Goodbye to Shame (Kendall), 164
self-pity, 57
slumber zone, 80
Sodom and Gomorrah, 20
success, 40, 93, 139
suicide, 82-84

T

Taylor, Jill Bolte, 183
Tina (friend of Dixon, Althea Lee), 166
Tiny (aunt of Dixon, Althea Lee), 19-20

V

vision, 80

W

When I Lay My Isaac Down (Kent), 144-45

Edwards Brothers,Inc!
Thorofare, NJ 08086
22 March, 2011
BA2011081